VOCABULARY
FROM
CLASSICAL ROOTS

B

Norma Fifer ▾ Nancy Flowers

Educators Publishing Service

Cambridge and Toronto

Acknowledgments

Illustrations in *Vocabulary from Classical Roots—B* have been taken from the following sources:

Catchpenny Prints. 163 Popular Engravings from the Eighteenth Century. New York: Dover Publications, Inc., 1970.

1800 Woodcuts by Thomas Bewick and His School. Blanche Cirker, ed. New York: Dover Publications, Inc., 1962.

Food and Drink. A Pictorial Archive from Nineteenth-Century Sources. Selected by Jim Harter. Third revised edition. New York: Dover Publications, Inc., 1983.

Harter's Picture Archive for Collage and Illustration. Jim Harter, ed. New York: Dover Publications, Inc., 1978.

Huber, Richard. *Treasury of Fantastic and Mythological Creatures. 1,087 Renderings from Historic Sources.* New York: Dover Publications, Inc., 1981.

The Illustrator's Handbook. Compiled by Harold H. Hart. New York: Galahad Books, 1978.

Men. A Pictorial Archive from Nineteenth-Century Sources. Selected by Jim Harter. New York: Dover Publications, Inc., 1980.

More Silhouettes. 868 Copyright-Free Illustrations for Artists and Craftsmen. Carol Belanger Grafton, ed. New York: Dover Publications, Inc., 1982.

1,001 Advertising Cuts from the Twenties and Thirties. Compiled and arranged by Leslie Carbarga, Richard Greene, and Marina Cruz. New York: Dover Publications, Inc. 1987.

Silhouettes. A Pictorial Archive of Varied Illustrations. Carol Belanger Grafton, ed. New York: Dover Publications, Inc., 1979.

Tierney, Tom. *Travel and Tourist Illustrations.* New York, Dover Publications, Inc., 1987.

2001 Decorative Cuts and Ornaments. Carol Belanger Grafton, ed. New York: Dover Publications, Inc., 1988.

Victorian Spot Illustrations, Alphabets and Ornaments from Porret's Type Catalog. Carol Belanger Grafton, ed. New York: Dover Publications, Inc., 1982.

Cover photograph by Photodisc/ Getty Images.

Printed in U.S.A.
ISBN 0-8388-2254-1

3 4 5 6 7 BRB 09 08 07 06 05

Contents

Preface

Vocabulary from Classical Roots encourages you to look at words as members of families in the way astronomers see stars as parts of constellations. Here you will become acquainted with constellations of words descended from Greek and Latin, visible in families that cluster around such subjects as the human being, kinds of mental activity, and aspects of daily life.

You will notice that Latin and Greek forms appear as complete words, not as fragments. Some alliances in word families are easily recognizable, but others may seem strange without your seeing the complete sequence of forms. Some Latin words are consistent in their basic forms, like *jocus*, "joke," but others shift in spelling according to the way they are used in Latin sentences: *ars, artis*, "art," and *iter, itineris*, "journey." The principal parts of the verb "to turn" are similar in form: *verso, versare, versavi, versatum*. But this regularity disappears in the verb "to bear": *fero, ferre, tuli, latum*. If you didn't know that these forms belong to one verb, would you believe that the English words *conference* and *relationship* belong to the family?

This book can do more than increase your recognition of words; perhaps it will encourage you to study Latin or Greek. More immediately, though, it can remind you that English is a metaphorical language. By returning to the origins of English words you will move closer to knowing how language began: in naming people, things, and concrete actions. So enjoy visualizing the life behind the words you use every day, descendants of Latin and Greek, seeming almost as numerous as stars.

Notes on Using *Vocabulary from Classical Roots*

1. **Latin (L.) and Greek (G.) forms.** Complete sets of these forms help to explain the spelling of their English derivatives. Practice pronouncing these words by following some simple rules.

   To pronounce Latin:
   Every *a* sounds like *ah,* as in *swan.*
   The letter *v* is pronounced like *w.*
   The letter *e* at the end of a word, as in the verb *negare,* should sound like the *e* in *egg.*

   To pronounce Greek:
   As in Latin, *a* sounds like *ah.*
   The diphthong *ei* rhymes with *say;* for example, the verb *agein* rhymes with *rain.*
   Au, as in *autos,* sounds like the *ow* in *owl,* and *os* rhymes with *gross.*

2. **Diacritical marks.** Following every defined word in *Vocabulary from Classical Roots* is the guide to pronunciation, as in (dī ə krĭt′ ĭ kəl). The letter that looks like an upside-down *e* (called a *schwa*) is pronounced like the *a* in *about.* You will find a key to the diacritical marks used in this book on the inside front cover.

3. **Derivation.** Information in brackets after the guide to pronunciation for a word gives further information about the source of that word. For example, after **diacritical** (dī ə krĭt′ ĭ kəl), under *dia* <G. "apart," would appear [*krinein* <G. "to separate"]. Thus, the word *diacritical* is made up of two words that come from Greek and means "separating the parts" and, consequently, "distinguishing."

4. **Familiar Words and Challenge Words.** Listed next to groups of defined words may be one or two sets of words belonging to the same family. You probably already know the Familiar Words in the shaded boxes. Try to figure out the meanings of the Challenge Words, and if you are curious, look them up in a dictionary.

5. **Nota Bene.** *Nota bene* means "note well" and is usually abbreviated to *N.B.* In *Vocabulary from Classical Roots,* NOTA BENE calls your attention informally to other words related to the theme of the lesson.

6. **Exercises.** The exercises help you determine how well you have learned the words in each lesson while also serving as practice for examinations such as the SAT: synonyms and antonyms, analogies, and sentence completions. Further exercises illustrate words used in sentences, test recognition of roots, and offer writing practice.

PART ONE

Action

Motion

Directions

1. Determine how the Latin or Greek root is related in meaning to each defined—KEY—word that follows it.
2. Learn the pronunciation and definition(s) of each KEY word, and notice how the words are used in sentences.
3. Practice using the varied forms of KEY words.
4. Build your knowledge with all the information given: Latin mottoes, Familiar Words, Challenge Words, and Nota Bene references.
5. Complete the exercises.

LESSON 1

Nolo contendere.
I do not wish to contend.*

Key Words		
contend	elation	perennial
defer	infer	permeate
dilatory	intent	perservere
	percussion	

*A legal term used when a defendant does not admit guilt but offers no defense.

Familiar Words
impervious
perceive
percent
perfect
perfume
permission
perpetual
perplex
persist
perspire

Challenge Words
imperturbable
perambulate
perigee
perpetuity
perspicacious
pertinacious
perturb
pervade
repercussion

PER <L. "through"

1. **percussion**   (pər kŭsh'ən)   [*cuss* = *quatere* <L. "to strike"]
   n. 1. The sharp striking of one thing against another.

   The familiar **percussion** of wood on leather let us know that baseball practice had begun.

   2. Instruments that make a sound when struck.

   Percussion in an orchestra includes drum, cymbals, tympani, xylophone, and piano.

   adj. Describing the striking of a substance or a musical instrument.

   Small children use kitchen pots and pans as **percussion** instruments.

   percussionist, *n.*; **percussive**, *adj.*

2. **perennial**   (pə rĕn'ē əl)   [*annus* <L. "year"]
   adj. 1. Lasting for an indefinitely long time.

   Mother Goose rhymes have remained **perennial** favorites with children.

   2. Continuing regularly.

   A **perennial** remark of parents is "Things were different when I was your age."

   3. Living longer than two years, said especially of plants.

   Perennial shrubs like roses and lilacs satisfy gardeners not only because they smell good, but also because they grow for many years.

   perennially, *adv.*

3. **permeate**   (pûr'mē āt´)   [*meare* <L. "to go," "to pass"]
   tr. v. To penetrate through spaces; to spread throughout.

   Pollution from automobiles and smokestacks **permeates** the air in many cities, causing health problems for people and contributing to the deterioration of the environment.

   permeable, *adj.*; **permeation**, *n.*
   Antonym: **impermeable**.

   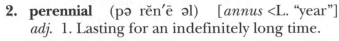

4. **persevere**   (pûr sə vĭr´)   [*serverus* <L. "severe," "serious"]
   intr. v. To hold fast to a task or purpose despite handicaps or obstacles.

Elizabeth Blackwell, the first woman doctor in the United States, **persevered** despite ridicule and exclusion from the medical profession.

perseverance, *n.*

FERO, FERRE, TULI, LATUM <L. "to bring," "to bear," "to carry"

Familiar Words
confer
differ
dilate
fertile
legislator
offer
prefer
refer
relate
suffer
transfer
translate

Challenge Words
collate
oblate
prelate
proffer
superlative
vociferous

5. **defer** (dĭ fûr´) [*de* <L. "away:]
tr. v. To postpone; to delay.

Schools and colleges sometimes **defer** admission, accepting students later in the year.

intr. v. To yield respectfully to the opinion or will of another.

When the rabbits in *Watership Down* plan their escape, they **defer** to Hazel, the wisest rabbit of the warren.

deference, *n.*; **deferential**, *adj.*; **deferentially**, *adv.*

6. **dilatory** (dĭl´ə tôr´ē) [*dis* <L. "apart"]
adj. Tending to delay or to postpone.

In one of Aesop's fables, the **dilatory** hare loses the race to the perserving tortoise.

dilatorily, *adj.*; **dilatoriness**, *n.*

7. **elation** (ī lā´shən) [*e* = *ex* <L. "from," "out of"]
n. Excited feelings of pride, triumph, or happiness.

Many Americans felt **elation** when two *Apollo* astronauts took their first steps on the moon in 1969.

elated, *adj.*

8. **infer** (ĭn fûr´) [*in* <L. "in"]
tr. v. 1. To use available evidence to form a conclusion.

The jury **inferred** from the testimony that the defendant was guilty.

2. To guess.

You can't **infer** that people have talent just because they are celebrities.

inference, *n.*; **inferential**, *adj.*; **inferentially**, *adv.*

NOTA BENE: Don't confuse *infer* with *imply*, which means "to hint," "to suggest," or "to mean." A person shows or says (*implies*) what another interprets (*infers*). For example: My teacher's comment *implies* that I have written a good paper; I *infer* that she thinks I have written a good paper.

Familiar Words
attend
detention
intense
pretend
tendency
tense
tension

Challenge Words
detente
entente
portend
tendentious

TENDO, TENDERE, TETENDI, TENSUM <L. "to stretch"

9. **contend**   (kən tĕnd´)   [*con* = *cum* <L. "with"]
   intr. v. 1. To engage in a quarrel, a struggle, or rivalry.

   Cyclists on the Tour de France **contend** not only with each other, but also with dehydration and fatigue.

   2. To assert; to put forward in argument.

   The doctor **contended** that all children should be vaccinated against polio.

   contender, *n.*; **contention**, *n.*; **contentious**, *adj.*; **contentiously**, *adv.*

10. **intent**   (ĭn tĕnt´)   [*in* <L. "in"]
    n. Purpose.

    The **intent** of Christopher Columbus was to find a new sea route to Asia from Europe; instead, he found a new continent.

    adj. Concentrating on or dedicated to an idea or action.

    Girls who were **intent** upon joining Little League teams won the right to do so in a 1974 court decree.

EXERCISE 1A

Circle the letter of the best SYNONYM (the word or phrase most nearly the same as the word in bold-faced type).

1. annual **contention** for the trophy   a. longing   b. rivalry   c. hope   d. vanguard   e. perseverance
2. to **permeate** the soil   a. cover   b. exist in   c. eliminate   d. contaminate   e. penetrate
3. **perseverance** in competitive sports   a. dabbling   b. winning   c. persistence   d. disinterest   e. pretentiousness

Circle the letter of the best ANTONYM (the word or phrase most nearly opposite the word in bold-faced type).

4. **perennial** problems   a. short-lived   b. annual   c. usual   d. long-lasting   e. unsolvable
5. a **dilatory** response to an invitation   a. thoughtful   b. prompt   c. half-hearted   d. quarrelsome   e. delayed
6. a moment of **elation**   a. excitement   b. exhaustion   c. humor   d. joy   e. sadness

7. **deferring** a hard decision   a. making   b. postponing   c. hastening
    d. challenging   e. rejecting
8. to **infer** the outcome   a. believe   b. learn   c. deny   d. imply
    e. guess at

EXERCISE 1B   Circle the letter of the sentence in which the word in bold-faced type is
used incorrectly.

1. a. In the poem "Harlem," Langston Hughes asks, "What happens to
        a dream **deferred**?" addressing the denial of opportunity
        experienced by many African Americans.
    b. Because Arachne, famous for her skill at the loom, refuses to
        defer to Minerva in a weaving contest, the goddess transforms
        her into a spider.
    c. The students apologized for the **deference** that made them tardy.
    d. A basic courtesy is **deference** of youth to age when entering a
        room or passing through a doorway.
2. a. Bamboo poles clapped on the floor provide the **percussion**
        accompaniment for the Filipino dance, "Singkil."
    b. Who can resist the rhythmic **percussion** of tap dancers?
    c. The complicated steps and rhythmic **percussion** of castanets
        require a flamenco dancer's full concentration.
    d. When workers go out on strike, they commit a **percussive** act.
3. a. China for centuries **contended** with Mongolian invaders from the
        north.
    b. A happy man, he lived in a state of perfect **contention**.
    c. *The Contender* is a novel about an African-American youth who
        wants to make a name for himself as a boxer.
    d. The U.S. Surgeon General has **contended** that people should
        safeguard their health by avoiding tobacco, alcohol, and harmful
        drugs.
4. a. Some scientists believe that massive amounts of dust **permeated**
        Earth's atmosphere after a collision with an asteroid, causing the
        extinction of the dinosaurs.
    b. The smell **permeating** our house could only be skunk.
    c. When the crowd heard that their candidate had won, feelings of
        elation **permeated** the hall.
    d. The toughness of leather makes it difficult to **permeate** with an
        ordinary needle.
5. a. Do you agree that the familiar phrase, "for all **intents** and
        purposes," is repetitious?
    b. On our camping trip we were prepared for a snug, **intent** night's
        sleep, but a prowling bear kept us awake.

  c. Although the **intent** of the Chinese students' demonstration in
   1989 was for free speech and control of corruption, the nation's
   leaders feared a movement to overthrow the government.

  d. Sarah Winnemucca was **intently** involved in pleading with the
   U.S. government for fair treatment of her people, the Paiutes.

6. a. When Izzy's best friends are **dilatory** in making a hospital visit
   after her injury, she realizes that they may not be her best friends
   after all.

  b. Sir Walter Scott once noted that unanswered letters are like
   snakes hissing at his **dilatoriness**.

  c. If their supervisor requires punctuality, **dilatory** employees are in
   danger of losing their jobs.

  d. We were driving in the **dilatory** lane because we were short of
   gas.

7. a. On August 14, 1945, **elated** throngs gathered to celebrate the
   official end of World War II.

  b. For Hank Aaron a day of **elation** came in 1974 when he hit his
   715th home run, breaking the lifetime record held by Babe Ruth.

  c. The envelope contained a small, neat **elation** with her name on it.

  d. Teacher Anne Sullivan's **elation** was great when Helen Keller,
   without sight or hearing, learned her first word—*water*.

8. a. The **perseverance** and hard work of Spanish-speaking Mexican
   immigrants were responsible for the prosperous economy of the
   Southwest in the nineteenth century.

  b. Rather than **persevere** dilatory staff members to meet deadlines,
   the editor coaxed them with prizes and treats.

  c. **Persevering** in her struggle for women's rights, attorney Belva
   Lockwood helped to get laws passed that gave women equal rights
   to property and child guardianship.

  d. Although the mythological character Sisyphus **perseveres** in
   pushing a huge boulder up a steep hill, his punishment is having
   it always roll back down.

EXERCISE 1C

Fill in each blank with the most appropriate word from Lesson 1. Use a
word or any of its forms only once.

1. From the smell of burned muffins issuing from the kitchen, we

  _____ that the cook will not be in a good mood.

2. The government penalizes citizens who are _____
  in paying their taxes.

3. Nellie Bly had cause for _____ after setting a new
  record: traveling around the world in fewer than the 80 days Phileas
  Fogg needed in Jules Verne's novel.

4. The _____ of the woodpecker drumming on a tree trunk signifies a search for insects or proclaims the bird's territory and readiness to mate.

5. "La Bamba," a song with numerous verses, has become a(n)

_____ favorite, continuing to reflect life in Mexican fishing villages.

6. The crew of the spaceship *Discovery* in the movie *2001: A Space Odyssey*

is _____ on finding proof that creatures from outer space influenced earth forms millions of years ago.

LESSON 2

Sub rosa.
Under the rose, or secretly.*

Key Words		
adversity	introvert	retort
avert	perverse	subservient
contort	prose	subvert
distort	tortuous	

Familiar Words
subdue
subject
sublime
submit
substance
substitute
subtraction
suburb
succeed

Challenge Words
subconscious
subjective
sublimate
subside
subterfuge
succumb

SUB <L. "under"

1. **subvert**   (səb vûrt´)   [*vertere* <L. "to turn"]
   tr. v. To upset; to overthrow; to ruin.

   In 1917 revolutionists **subverted** the regime of the Russian czars.

   subversion, *n.*; **subversive**, *adj.*; **subverted**, *adj.*

2. **subservient**   (səb sər´vĭ ənt)
   [*servare* <L. "to serve"]
   adj. Excessively willing to yield; submissive.

   History shows that although men have often expected women to be **subservient**, many women have resisted domination.

   subservience, *n.*; **subserviently**, *adv.*

*The rose is a classical symbol of secrecy.

TORQUEO, TORQUERE, TORSI, TORTUM <L. "to twist," "to bend," "to turn around"

3. **contort**   (kən tôrt′)   [con = cum <L. "with"]
   tr. v. To twist or bend out of shape.

   The acrobats **contorted** their bodies until they resembled pretzels.

   contorted, *adj.*; **contortion**, *n.*

4. **distort**   (dĭs tôrt′)   [dis <L. "apart"]
   tr. v. 1. To change something to make it false.

   By combining photographs of two people who have never met, a devious propagandist could **distort** their relationship and mislead the public.

   2. To twist (something) out of its natural shape.

   Both heat and dampness can **distort** videocassettes and computer disks.

5. **retort**   (rĭ tôrt′)   [re <L. "back," "again"]
   tr. and *intr. v.* To reply quickly and sharply, often as if in reply to an accusation.

   When the ventriloquist told her dummy, "You're not very bright today," the figure **retorted**, "Look who's talking."

   n. A quick, witty, sometimes biting reply.

   In the television series *M*A*S*H*, "Hawkeye" Pierce is known for **retorts** that show his frustrations with life in a temporary army hospital during the war in Korea.

6. **tortuous**   (tôr′cho͞o əs)
   adj. 1. Having many twists and turns.

   Three animals make a **tortuous** return to their owners in the story *The Incredible Journey*.

   2. Deceitfully roundabout; tricky.

   Tom Sawyer's **tortuous** plan to free Jim, the already freed former slave, becomes a hardship, or at least a nuisance, to everyone except Tom.

   tortuously, *adv.*; **tortuousness**, *n.*

   NOTA BENE: The word *torturous* comes from the same Latin word as *tortuous* but, as the adjective form of *torture*, is much stronger in meaning: "causing torture" or "causing mental suffering."

Familiar Words
advertisement
anniversary
controversy
convert
divert
invert
revert
universe
versatile
verse
version
vice versa

Challenge Words
extroversion
vertebra
vertigo
vortex

VERSO, VERSARE, VERSAVI, VERSATUM <L. "to turn," "to turn around"

7. **adversity** (ăd vûr′sə tē) [ad <L. "to," "toward]
   n. Hardship; misfortune.

   Despite the **adversity** of a shipwreck, the Swiss Family Robinson adapts to living simply, turning their island into a small paradise.

   adverse, *adj.*; **adversely**, *adv.*

8. **avert** (ə vûrt′) [a = ab <L. "away from"]
   tr. v. To turn away (one's eyes).

   During an eclipse of the sun, viewers must **avert** their eyes to avoid severe burning of the retina.

   2. To prevent.

   Although the hydraulic system of the plane was gone, the pilot **averted** total disaster in landing.

   averted, *adj.*

9. **introvert** (ĭn′trə vûrt) [*intro* <L. "within," "inward"]
   n. A person whose thoughts and interests are directed inward.

   Introverts often keep extensive journals, in which they record their thoughts about life.

   introversion, *n.*; **introverted**, *adj.*

10. **perverse** (pər vûrs′) [*per* <L. "through"]
    adj. Stubbornly doing something other than what is reasonable or required.

    The children took **perverse** pleasure in hiding from their sitter.

    perversely, *adv.*; **perverseness**, *n.*; **perversity**, *n.*

11. **prose** (prōz)
    [*prosa* <L. "straightforward" from *proversum* <L. "turned forward"]
    n. Ordinary speech or writing without rhyme or meter (that is, without verse).

    Prose is what we all speak and write unless we are composing poetry.

    adj. Referring to speech or writing other than verse.

    Laura Ingall Wilder's **prose** style makes life on the American frontier quickly accessible to her readers.

    prosaic, *adj.*

EXERCISE 2A   Circle the letter of the best SYNONYM (the word or phrase most nearly the same as the word in bold-faced type).

1. hopeful even in **adversity**   a. good fortune   b. fame   c. change
    d. hard times   e. discomfort
2. **subversion** of an enterprise   a. concealment   b. support
    c. celebration   d. annihilation   e. aberration
3. **distortion** of the facts   a. alteration   b. description
    c. recantation   d. clarification   e. salience
4. **introverted** attitudes   a. outgoing   b. self-confident
    c. capricious   d. selfish   e. inward-looking

Circle the letter of the best ANTONYM (the word or phrase most nearly opposite the word in bold-faced type).

5. to **avert** disaster   a. consider   b. anticipate   c. encounter
    d. prevent   e. enjoy
6. **perverse** responses   a. lively   b. wicked   c. reasonable
    d. tortuous   e. prose
7. **contorted** metal sculpture   a. rounded   b. twisted   c. piled
    d. straightened   e. ugly
8. to adopt a **subservient** manner   a. helpful   b. submissive
    c. reverent   d. suspicious   e. bullying

EXERCISE 2B   Circle the letter of the sentence in which the word in bold-faced type is used incorrectly.

1. a. Adventure games on computers sometimes require players to
        follow **tortuous** routes to solve the puzzle and find the treasure.
    b. Forcing **tortuous** misunderstanding, Little Buttercup at last
        reveals the identity of her marriageable son in *H.M.S. Pinafore*.
    c. Agatha Christie's mystery stories promise **tortuous** plots before
        the detective nabs the wrongdoer.
    d. The prisoners suffered severe **tortuousness** from their cruel
        captors.
2. a. We discussed the **prose** and cons of turbo engines.
    b. Edgar Allen Poe wrote both poetry and **prose**.
    c. Trying to smarten himself up to become a gentleman, a character
        in a French play is amazed when his tutor tells him he has been
        speaking **prose** all his life.
    d. In *Charlie and the Chocolate Factory*, a scolding voice speaking in
        rhyme sometimes interrupts the **prose**.

3. a. The poem contained many stanzas because the poet expected to be paid on a **perverse** basis.
    b. The **perverseness** of the princess who complains about the pea under her twenty-four mattresses shows a delicate sensitivity that wins her a princely bridegroom.
    c. Nature sometimes appears **perverse**, sending flash floods to drown thousands in Bangladesh while the land dries up in the famine-stricken Sahara.
    d. Although Templeton the rat is often **perverse** when Charlotte the spider asks a favor, he manages to save the day on several occasions in the story *Charlotte's Web*.

4. a. Historian Elizabeth Longford writes that "as playthings or household slaves, women were **distorted** the world over."
    b. Makeup and padding **distorted** the figure of Charles Laughton for his role in the film *The Hunchback of Notre Dame*.
    c. Clowns tumbling from the diving board entertained the audience with their **distortions**.
    d. Under the leadership of Joseph Stalin and his successors, Russian history presented as truth many **distortions** and omissions of world events.

5. a. The team crossing Antarctica by sled placed trust in the lead dog to **avert** dangerous crevasses.
    b. Writers often **avert** to their own experience in both prose and poetry.
    c. In some cultures politeness requires **averting** the eyes rather than looking directly at someone.
    d. By breaking German codes during World War II, British forces could **avert** some damage by preparing for air attack.

6. a. We often think of a good **retort** too late to use it.
    b. In *Pride and Prejudice* Elizabeth Bennet **retorts** to the haughty Lady Catherine, who delivers a **retort** in return: "I send no compliments to your mother."
    c. "Really?" and "You know?" are **retorts** we often hear in conversation.
    d. When Mrs. Hardcastle in the play *She Stoops to Conquer* scolds her son for playing a trick on her, he **retorts**, "Ecod, mother, all the parish says you spoiled me, and so you may take the fruits on it."

7. a. Despite the gardener's perseverance in planting parsley, a hungry vole **subverted** all of her efforts.
    b. Socrates was put to death for supposedly **subverting** the minds of Athenian youth by teaching them to reason.
    c. In 1917 the French government tried and executed Mata Hari for **subversion**: conveying military secrets to the Germans.
    d. The speaker declared that racism still exists; it has only been **subverted** from our attention.

8. a. In the Middle Ages serfs were bound in **subservience** to their lord.
    b. At the Constitutional Convention in 1787 the idea of being **subservient** to a national rather than a state government frightened some of the framers of the Constitution.
    c. On a plantation the **subservients** who worked in the fields had a more difficult life than those skilled in a craft.
    d. Although seeming **subservient** to the new regime, the people quietly resisted.

EXERCISE 2C   Fill in each blank with the most appropriate word from Lesson 2. Use a word or any of its forms only once.

1. Balancing a budget is a(n) _____ task for individuals as well as for governments.
2. When several people pass along information one by one, they inevitably _____ it.
3. Although admirers were eager to lionize the Brontë sisters, they were _____s, preferring their own company to that of the outside world.

4. Thomas Carlyle says that "_____ is hard upon a man" but that prosperity is even harder to endure.

5. A clever _____ may win admiration for wit but discourage gentler feelings.

6. Readers of Beverly Cleary's _____ have met Henry Huggins, an amusing character who appears in a succession of her novels.

7. As they leap, turn somersaults, and otherwise _____ their bodies, Olympic gymnasts prove their suppleness.
8. Although the nursery rhyme begins, "Mary, Mary, quite contrary," the references to her garden and "maids all in a row" do not explain why she is _____.

REVIEW EXERCISES FOR LESSONS 1 AND 2

1 Fill in the blanks or circle the letter of the best answer.

1. Which of the following English words does *not* derive from a Latin verb meaning "to twist" or "to turn"?
   a. tortuous   b. subvert   c. contort   d. dilatory   e. perverse
2. The words *confer, relate, prefer,* and *translate* come from the Latin

   verb _____, meaning _____.

3. *per* : through : : *sub* : _____
4. The words *contend, intent, attention,* and *tense* come from the Latin

   verb _____, meaning _____.

5. perennial : long-lasting : :
   a. perverse : agreeable
   b. introverted : outgoing
   c. dilatory : ready
   d. elated : happy
   e. percussive : silent

2 Matching: On the line at the left, write the letter of the word or phrase that most accurately defines the word in the left-hand column.

_____	1. introversion	A. hardship
_____	2. percussion	B. determination
_____	3. deference	C. disagreement
_____	4. contortion	D. sound of striking
_____	5. dilatoriness	E. inwardness
_____	6. elation	F. tardiness
_____	7. adversity	G. respect
_____	8. contention	H. stubbornness
_____	9. perseverance	I. joy
_____	10. perversity	J. twisting

3   Writing or Discussion Activities

1. In a brief paragraph describe a situation in which you felt *elation.* What are the reasons you experienced this feeling? In your paragraph give specific details allowing your reader to visualize the moment (who? what? when? where?). Use *elation* or *elated* in at least one of your sentences.

2. One of the most irregular verbs in Latin is *fero, ferre, tuli, latum.* Think of a way to remember this odd verb with its unmatching parts, and explain in a few sentences how you will go about keeping it in mind, along with some of its useful derivatives.

3. Imagine yourself at a circus, watching acrobats, clowns, musicians, and animals perform. From the list of words below choose at least four to use in a brief paragraph in which you describe the sights, sounds, and smells under the big top. Use the form of the word that best expresses your idea.

percussion	contortion	avert	perverse
permeate	retort	infer	persevere
contend			tortuous

Position

LESSON 3

Nihil legebat quod non excerperet.
He read nothing from which he did not pluck something.
—PLINY THE YOUNGER

Key Words		
compound	exonerate	impose
excerpt	exorbitant	impostor
exhilarate	exposition	proponent
	expound	

EX <L. "from," "out of"

1. **excerpt** (ĕk′sûrpt) [*carpere* <L. "to pick," "to pluck," "to seize"] *n.* A passage selected from a book, play, piece of music, etc.

   Our anthology contains thousands of **excerpts** from literature around the world.

   tr. v. To take a passage from a book, etc.; to quote.

   The students **excerpted** their favorite numbers from *Cats* to perform at the variety show.

2. **exhilarate** (ĕg zĭl′ə rāt, ĭg zĭl′ə rāt)
[*hilaris* <L. "cheerful," "happy";
hilaros <G. "cheerful," "happy"]
tr. v. To cheer; to stimulate; to enliven.

Her critically acclaimed performance at the opening of the 1961 season of the Metropolitan Opera must have **exhilarated** Leontyne Price.

exhilarated, *adj.*; **exhilarating**, *adj.*; **exhilaration**, *n.*

3. **exonerate** (ĕg zŏn′ə rāt)   [*onus* <L. "burden," "load"]
tr. v. 1. To free from blame.

When new evidence **exonerated** the accused forger, the bank president reinstated him at a higher salary.

2. To relieve of a task.

As a reward for their hours of babysitting, their parents **exonerated** them from mowing the lawn.

exonerated, *adj.*; **exoneration**, *n.*

4. **exorbitant** (ĕg zōr′bə tənt, ĭg zôr′bə tənt)   [*orbita* <L. "route"]
adj. Excessive.

The rhinoceros is in danger of becoming extinct because of the **exorbitant** price poachers receive for the animals' horns.

exorbitance, *n.*; **exorbitancy**, *n.*; **exorbitantly**, *adv.*

PONO, PONERE, POSUI, POSITUM <L. "to place," "to put"

5. **compound** (kŏm pound′)   [*com = cum* <L. "with," "together"]
tr. v. To mix together; to combine two or more parts or elements.

The Kirov Ballet of the former Soviet Union **compounded** its traditional style with contemporary music and dance from other countries.

adj. (kŏm′pound) Having two or more parts or elements.

A **compound** sentence has two or more main clauses, as in "We ran fast, but they caught us."

n. A combination of elements, parts, or substances.

Steel is a **compound**, or alloy, of iron, carbon, and other substances such as copper, cobalt, and silicon.

6. **exposition**   (ĕkʹ spə zĭshʹən)   [*ex* <L. "from," "out of"]
   n. 1. A precise statement or explanation.

   With both written text and 1,065 colored illustrations, John James Audubon's *Birds of America*, published in 1838, remains a model **exposition** on the subject.

   2. A public exhibit or show.

   The first international **exposition** was held in London's Crystal Palace in 1851.

   expository, *adj.*

7. **expound**   (ĕk spoundʹ, ĭk spoundʹ)   [*ex* <L. "from," "out of"]
   tr. and *intr. v.* To set forth an explanation or view of something in detail (usually used with *on*).

   The travelers **expounded** on the animals they saw on their safari in Kenya.

8. **impose**   (ĭm pōzʹ)   [*im = in* <L. "in"]
   tr. v. To set up, or to force something (or oneself) on others.

   Under apartheid, the South African government **imposed** laws that granted different rights to people based on the color of their skin.

   intr. v. To take unfair advantage of someone.

   In the play *The Man Who Came to Dinner*, a guest who breaks his hip when departing **imposes** on his hosts for six months.

   imposed, *adj.*; **imposition**, *n.*

   NOTA BENE: The adjective *imposing* has a different meaning from the forms given above, a favorable one: "impressive" and "awe-inspiring." For example, An *imposing* figure physically, Paul Robeson was even more impressive for his talents as scholar, athlete, actor, and singer.

9. **impostor**   (ĭm pŏsʹtər)   [*im = in* <L. "in"]
   n. One who deceives by using a false identity.

   The wife of Martin Guerre wonders if the man claiming to be Martin is really her husband returning after eight years or an **impostor**.

10. **proponent**   (prə pōʹnənt)   [*pro* <G. "before"]
    n. One who argues in support of something.

    Proponents of recycling newsprint, glass, and aluminum have found citizens more willing to cooperate than they expected.

    Antonym: **opponent**

EXERCISE 3A   Circle the letter of the best SYNONYM (the word or phrase most nearly the same as the word(s) in bold-faced type).

1. **excerpts from** an opera   a. artifices in   b. characters in
   c. omissions from   d. plots in   e. portions of
2. to **expound on** one's success   a. relive   b. underestimate
   c. explain in detail   d. brag about   e. subvert
3. **exoneration** of an offender   a. disbelief   b. pursuit
   c. condemnation   d. release   e. imprisonment
4. **imposition** of a hardship   a. infliction   b. removal
   c. endurance   d. defense   e. annihilation

Circle the letter of the best ANTONYM (the word or phrase most nearly opposite the word in bold-faced type).

5. **exhilarating** evenings   a. depressing   b. cheering   c. tiring
   d. unremarkable   e. primordial
6. a(n) **proponent** of a vegetarian diet   a. example   b. opponent
   c. enthusiast   d. inventor   e. interpreter
7. **exorbitant** fees   a. reasonable   b. precise   c. excessive   d. basic
   e. very low

EXERCISE 3B   Circle the letter of the sentence in which the word in bold-faced type is used incorrectly.

1. a. Although a creator and **proponent** of the atomic bomb, Robert Oppenheimer became an opponent of its use.
   b. Cinderella becomes the **proponent** character in the fairy tale when the matching slipper fits her foot rather than those of her stepsisters.
   c. Growing up poor and having no formal education, President Andrew Johnson became an enthusiastic **proponent** of public schools.
   d. Mother Jones was such a vocal **proponent** of child labor laws and concern for the poor that she sometimes went to jail for her beliefs.
2. a. Through friendship with James II, the English king, William Penn managed to arrange **exoneration** of religious prisoners.
   b. Some food specialists have **exonerated** chocolate as the cause of headaches and acne.
   c. Enrolling in a cooking class **exonerated** her from her dream of becoming a chef.
   d. Falsely accused of treason and imprisoned on Devil's Island, Captain Alfred Dreyfus received full **exoneration** after Emile Zola and others challenged the verdict.

3. a. Before she was eighteen Adela Rogers St. Johns was **expounding** on the "police beat, sports, sin, and society" for a daily newspaper.
   b. When baseball fans start talking about teams and heroes, they can **expound** all night.
   c. I have a math test; **expound** me on quadratic equations.
   d. Although shy, the artist was willing to **expound** upon her watercolors displayed in the exposition.

4. a. **Excerpts** of clothing were strewn around the room.
   b. In the drum and bugle corps competition, the champions performed **excerpts** from *The Phantom of the Opera*.
   c. Before copyright laws, people **excerpted** freely from the work of others without acknowledging authorship.
   d. A preacher's homily, or sermon, often contains **excerpts** from religious and literary works.

5. a. Set to music, the poem "Lift Every Voice and Sing" has become an **exhilarating** African American national anthem.
   b. **Exhilarating** vigorously, the tourists described the eerie emptiness of the Black Hills of South Dakota and their escape from the forest fire that swept through Yellowstone National Park.
   c. Sea literature contains many scenes of sailors **exhilarated** by riding the waves with wind-filled sails.
   d. After returning from the North Pole, Admiral Robert Peary wrote that "**exhilaration** of success lent wings to our sorely battered feet."

6. a. Although the Russian Dowager Empress accepted the self-proclaimed Anastasia as her granddaughter, most people believed her to be an **impostor**.
   b. Rudyard Kipling says, "If you can meet with Triumph and Disaster/ And treat those two **impostors** just the same," you show good judgment.
   c. Performers who substitute for actors in scenes requiring dangerous stunts are called **impostors**.
   d. A successful **impostor**, Deborah Sampson passed as an infantry volunteer for eighteen months during the Revolutionary War without being detected.

7. a. José Orozco was invited in 1940 to paint a mural for the Golden Gate International **Exposition** in San Francisco.
   b. A complex **exposition** by the physicist Stephen Hawking shows that the way the universe began is determined by the laws of science.
   c. Her carefully chosen **exposition** offered an excellent view of the stage.
   d. Although complete records of eating habits are rare, one Franciscan friar offers **expository** proof, with recipes, that Aztec noblemen in the sixteenth century ate tortillas every day.

8. a. The damage done by Hurricane Hugo was **compounded** by the simultaneous arrival of high tides.
    b. The skier's **compound** fracture of the tibia will require more time to mend than would a clean break.
    c. The hacienda in Latin American countries, like the plantation in the American South, is a **compound** of buildings for living, working, and storing supplies.
    d. A baker develops muscular strength through years of **compounding** bread dough.

EXERCISE 3C   Fill in each blank with the most appropriate word from Lesson 3. Use a word or any of its forms only once.

1. The _____ cost of houses in some parts of the country makes purchase of a first home difficult for many families.

2. Makers of perfume create a(n) _____ of oils from flowers and other plants, animal substances such as musk (from deer), alcohol, and water.

3. A frequently quoted _____ from Shakespeare begins, "All the world's a stage,/ And all the men and women merely players."

4. The coloration of the scorpionfish turns it into a successful

    _____: it appears to be a lump of coral before gulping down its unsuspecting prey.

5. Charged with faithlessness to her finance, Hero is fully

    _____d when the misunderstanding is explained in the play *Much Ado about Nothing*.

6. The _____ essay is a form students will often practice, especially if they plan to attend college.

7. As actors gain experience and prestige, they can more forcefully

    _____ their wills upon directors of plays and films.

LESSON 4

In medias res.
In the middle (the thick) of things.—HORACE

Key Words

extraneous	mediate	obsequious
extraterrestrial	mediocrity	sequester
extrovert	medium	subsequent
	non sequitur	

Familiar Words
extracurricular
extramural
extraordinary
extrasensory
extravagant
extravaganza

Challenge Words
extragalactic
extrajudicial
extraterritorial

EXTRA <L. "on the outside"

1. **extraneous**   (ĕk strā′nē əs)
   adj. 1. Coming from outside; foreign.

   To study a virus, laboratory technicians must remove all **extraneous** matter.

   2. Not essential or vital.

   Our history teacher said, "Keep to the subject; no **extraneous** details, please."

2. **extraterrestrial**   (ĕk strə tər əs′trē əl)   [*terra* <L. "earth"]
   adj. Outside or originating outside the limits of the earth's atmosphere.

   According to some scientists, the impact of an **extraterrestrial** object, such as a comet, caused conditions that led to the extinction of dinosaurs.

3. **extrovert**   (ĕks trə vûrt)   Also **extravert**.   [*vertere* <L. "to turn"]
   n. A person chiefly interested in things outside the self, directing thoughts outward rather inward.

   Some **extroverts** express their social ease with facile talk and colorful clothing.

   extroverted, *adj.*
   Antonym: **introvert**

MEDIUS <L. "middle"

4. **mediate**   (mē′dē āt′)
tr. v. To act as negotiator between opposing sides in a dispute.

During his presidency Jimmy Carter **mediated** disagreements between Israel and Egypt.

mediation, *n.*; **mediator**, *n.*

5. **mediocrity**   (mē′dē ŏk′rə tē)
n. The condition of being commonplace or ordinary, somewhere in the middle between high and low; a very ordinary person.

Although twice elected prime minister of Great Britain, Sir Winston Churchill was considered an academic **mediocrity** as a schoolboy.

mediocre, *adj.*

6. **medium**   (mē′dē əm; plural **media**: mē′dē ə)
n. 1. A substance or element through which something is transmitted.

For the Watusi, an African ethnic group, cattle are wealth and therefore become a **medium** of exchange.

2. A person thought to have communication with spirits of the dead.

Despite her implied powers as a **medium**, Madam Arcati cannot control the ghost of a first wife who complicates the lives of her successor and her helpless husband in the play *Blithe Spirit*.

NOTA BENE: Of course, *medium* also means "a condition halfway between extremes" (n.): Orange is the *medium* between yellow and red; (adj.): We sought a house in a *medium* price range.

SEQUOR, SEQUI, SECUTUM <L. "to follow"

7. **non sequitur**   (nŏn sĕk′wĭ tŏōr′)
[*non sequitur* <L. "it does not follow"]
n. A statement that does not follow logically from evidence.

"A person who cries must be sad" is a **non sequitur** because there are other reasons for tears than feeling sad: laughing uncontrollably and peeling onions, for example.

Challenge Words
ensue
inconsequential
sequestrate

NOTA BENE: A deliberate non sequitur can be a comic device, as humorist Robert Benchley illustrates:

"Is life too easy for youth of today? Are we raising a generation of pampered dawdlers? What is that on your necktie?

8. **obsequious** (əb sē′kwē əs) [*ob* <L. "to"]
adj. Excessively willing to yield to others.

The powerful Japanese military dictators known as shōguns expected their followers to be **obsequious**.

obsequiously, *adv.*; **obsequiousness**, *n.*

9. **subsequent** (sŭb′sə kwənt) [*sub* <L. "under"]
adj. Coming after or later.

After the volcano erupted, geologists carefully monitored **subsequent** rumblings.

subsequently, *adv.*

10. **sequester** (sə kwĕs′tər)
tr. v. 1. To go into hiding; to seek solitude.

Bears **sequester** themselves during the months of hibernation, sleeping through the winter.

2. To isolate.

Fearful of invasion during World War II, the U.S. government hastily **sequestered** American citizens of Japanese ancestry behind barbed wire in internment camps, an action now severely criticized.

sequestered, *adj.*; **sequestration**, *n.*

EXERCISE 4A

Circle the letter of the best SYNONYM (the word or phrase most nearly the same as the word in bold-faced type).

1. **obsequious** admirers   a. annoying   b. bossy   c. too subservient
   d. mimicking   e. pretentious
2. **mediation** of a conflict   a. stimulation   b. definition
   c. observation   d. circumvention   e. solution
3. a series of **mediocre** jobs   a. low-paying   b. outstanding
   c. central   d. undemanding   e. ordinary

Circle the letter of the best ANTONYM (the word or phrase most nearly opposite the word(s) in bold-faced type).

4. **subsequent** events   a. preceding   b. revealed   c. hidden
   d. following   e. recurring

5. famous for **non sequiturs**   a. brilliant expositions   b. illogical
    utterances   c. artful connections   d. cruel impositions
    e. extraverted remarks
6. **extraterrestrial** visitors   a. earthdwelling   b. ghostly
    c. unwelcome   d. heavenly   e. perverse
7. **extraneous** bits in the cereal   a. extra   b. essential   c. minute
    d. foreign   e. indigestible

EXERCISE 4B   Circle the letter of the sentence in which the word in bold-faced type is
used incorrectly.

1. a. French is the **extraneous** language that I study in school.
    b. The soprano added **extraneous** flourishes to her aria.
    c. We stretched the stew to feed **extraneous** guests.
    d. Smart mountain climbers put nothing **extraneous** in their
       backpacks.
2. a. Sea turtles **sequester** their eggs in sand, laboriously digging out a
       nest and keeping watch until the nestlings crack their shells and
       creep to the sea.
    b. Amish folk **sequester** themselves from influences they consider
       corrupting, such as automobiles and television.
    c. Crowds **sequestering** at Coney Island on hot summer days stroll
       along the boardwalk and swim in the Atlantic Ocean.
    d. Convents are places of **sequestration** so that women with a
       religious vocation can devote their energies to contemplation.
3. a. The movie *E.T.* shows the development of friendship between a
       human family and an **extraterrestrial** being.
    b. Although the pole quivered, it did not fall as a high jumper set
       a new record with an **extraterrestrial** leap of eight feet.
    c. In 1938 a radio production of Orson Welles's *War of the Worlds*
       sounded so real that many listeners believed an **extraterrestrial**
       invasion was occurring.
    d. The first woman to experience **extraterrestrial** flight, Valentina
       Tereshkova, described the horizon as "a light blue, a blue band."
4. a. During the Watergate investigation in the 1970s an important
       medium of information was someone known only as "Deep
       Throat."
    b. Many voters think the **media** should not project winners in a
       national election before the closing of all voting places.
    c. Some people's happy **medium** is gossip.
    d. Through the **medium** of a camera lens Marguerite Higgins
       caught images of war in Korea and Vietnam.

5. a. A rebellious **extrovert**, Isadora Duncan defend contemporary social conventions by dancing barefoot in gauze togas.
   b. If an **extrovert** is willing to look silly in public for comic effect, then Lucille Ball was an **extrovert**.
   c. The **extroverted** P.T. Barnum had the knack of gathering curiosities for his sideshows and delivering sales pitches that packed his circus tents with eager customers.
   d. The sign of an **extrovert** is greed, always wanting something extraneous.

EXERCISE 4C   Fill in each blank with the most appropriate word from Lesson 4. Use a word or any of its forms only once.

1. Exploring _____ phenomena gives astronomers clues to the millions of galaxies in the universe.

2. At first considered a(n) _____ in the art world, Consuelo Gonzáles Amézcua has achieved distinction for her pictures drawn with colored ball-point pens on cardboard.

3. To say that she is not a sensitive person because she doesn't like dogs is to use a(n) _____.

4. Organizations like Al-Anon provide trained people to

   _____ in cases of family conflict.

5. The satellite serves as a(n) _____ of information about weather, alerting watchers to storms and atmospheric aberrations around the globe.

6. Although the larval stage of the dragonfly may last for five years,

   the _____ stage as a gauzy-winged adult is brief, lasting perhaps five weeks.

7. Records of Dolley Madison's elegant gowns and large parties, when as the president's wife she was a White House hostess, strongly

   suggest that she was a(n) _____.

8. For centuries before the discovery of treatment for leprosy, sufferers of the disease lived as social outcasts,

   _____ed in remote colonies.

9. When expected to converse with a celebrity, some people become

   tongue-tied and _____, especially if they are taken by surprise.

REVIEW EXERCISES FOR LESSONS 3 AND 4

1   Circle the letter of the best answer to the following analogies.

1. *ponere* : *sequi* : :
   a. to flee : to serve
   b. to place : to follow
   c. to burden : to follow
   d. to place : to turn
   e. to stretch : to carry
2. obsequious : subservient : :
   a. impostor : truthful
   b. exorbitant : excessive
   c. mediocre : outstanding
   d. expound : remain silent
   e. subsequent : previous

2   Matching: On the line at the left, write the letter of the word with the same meaning as the prefix in the left-hand column.

_____	**1.** *extra* as in *extraneous*	A. under
_____	**2.** *sub* as in *subsequent*	B. before
_____	**3.** *ex* as in *excerpt*	C. from
_____	**4.** *in* as in *impose*	D. with
_____	**5.** *cum* as in compound	E. in
_____	**6.** *pro* as in *proponent*	F. outside

3   Writing or Discussion Activities

1. Which of the words listed below can best be used to describe an *extrovert?* Select three that seem the most appropriate to you. Justify your choice by writing a sentence for each, giving particular details that explain what an *extrovert* might do or say.

   compound   expound   mediate
   exhilarate   proponent   impose

2. If you were to read the following headlines in the newspaper, what would each one tell you? For each headline, write a short paragraph that explains what might be happening. Be imaginative in giving colorful details. If you need a model for such a paragraph, find an example in your daily newspaper.
   a. Subsequent Discoveries Exonerate Impostor
   b. Proponent of Exposition Confesses Mediocrity
   c. Extraneous Buildings Impose Exorbitant Cost

LESSONS 5 AND 6

Joining

LESSON 5

Modus vivendi.
A way of living (getting along).

+---+
| **Key Words** |
| abstain   commiserate   impertinent |
| coherent   commodious   pertinacious |
| colloquial   condone   tenacity |
| contrite |
+---+

CUM <L. "with," "together with"

NOTA BENE: In English, words derived from *cum* almost never use classical spelling; through time, sounds have changed to make pronunciation easier, and spellings have changed as well. *Cum* has become *co*, often with the addition of *l, m, n,* or *r,* as the following examples illustrate:

before vowels, *h, gn*	*co*	*coincide, cohesion*
before *l*	*co + l*	*collect, collide*
before *b, f, m, p*	*co + m*	*combine, compare*
before *r*	*co + r*	*correct, correspond*
before all other consonants	*co + n*	*concur, contain*

1. **coherent**   (kō hêr′ənt, kō hĕr′ənt)   [*haerere* <L. "to stick to"]
adj. 1. Showing an orderly relation of parts.

The play *Oedipus the King* is a model of **coherent** plot development, having a single line of action that takes place in one day.

2. Sticking together.

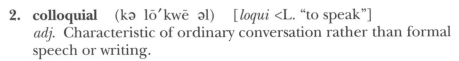

A honeycomb is a **coherent** structure of beeswax and honey.

cohere, *v.*; **coherence**, *n.*
Antonym: **incoherent**

2. **colloquial**   (kə lō′kwē əl)   [*loqui* <L. "to speak"]
adj. Characteristic of ordinary conversation rather than formal speech or writing.

"Let's stick together" is **colloquial**; "Let us be a coherent group" is formal.

colloquialism, *n.*; **colloquially**, *adv.*

3. **commiserate**   (kə mĭz′ə rāt)
[*miser* <L. "miserable," "wretched"]
tr. and *intr. v.* To feel or express sorrow or pity (used with *with*).

Following the assassination of President Kennedy in 1963, hundreds of people sent poems and letters to newspapers as a way to **commiserate** with the nation.

commiseration, *n.*

4. **condone**   (kən dōn′)   [*donum* <L. "gift"]
tr. v. To forgive; to disregard an offense.

The Ohlone people do not **condone** archaeologists' disturbing ancestral bones in tribal burying grounds.

5. **commodious**   (kə mō′dē əs)
[*modus* <L. "measure"]
adj. Spacious, roomy, as in a house.

Mount Vernon, George Washington's house on the Potomac River, is a **commodious** dwelling, having spacious rooms with high ceilings.

commodiously, *adv.*; **commodiousness**, *n.*

6. **contrite** (kən trīt′, kŏn′trīt) [*terere* <L. "to grind," "to tear away"]
adj. Thoroughly remorseful and repentant of one's sins.

According to Psalm 51 in the Bible, God looks with tolerance upon a sinner's "broken and **contrite** heart."

contrition, *n.*

TENEO, TENERE, TENUI, TENTUM <L. "to hold," "to keep"

7. **abstain** (ăb stān′) [*ab* <L. "away from"]
intr. v. To refrain from something by one's choice.

Doctors advise pregnant women to **abstain** from smoking and drinking alcoholic beverages, which can damage the fetus.

abstention, *n.*; **abstinence**, *n.*; **abstinent**, *adj.*

8. **impertinent** (ĭm pûrt′n ənt) [*im* = *in* <L. "not"]
adj. 1. Impudent; rude.

When in *Alice in Wonderland* the Cheshire Cat says he'd rather not kiss the hand of the King, that monarch replies, "Don't be **impertinent**."

2. Irrelevant.

A description of a scientific experiment avoids such **impertinent** information as personal opinion.

impertinence, *n.*; **impertinently**, *adv.*

9. **pertinacious** (pûr tə nā′shəs) [*per* <L. "through"]
adj. Holding firmly, even stubbornly, to a belief.

A **pertinacious** crusader against slavery and for women's rights, Sojourner Truth transfixed audiences with her message and her gospel singing.

pertinacity, *n.*; **pertinaciously**, *adv.*

10. **tenacity** (tə năs′ə tē)
n. Hanging on to something persistently or stubbornly.

Having lost the golf tournament, the seasoned champion showed her **tenacity** when she said, "I'll be back next year."

tenacious, *adj.*; **tenaciously**, *adv.*

Familiar Words
contain
content
contents
continent
continue
detain
discontented
entertain
lieutenant
maintain
obtain
pertain
retain
retainer
retention
sustain
tennis
tenor

Challenge Words
Continental
  Congress
continuum
continuity
sustenance
tenable
untenable

EXERCISE 5A   Circle the letter of the best SYNONYM (the word or phrase most nearly the same as the word in bold-faced type).

1. **contrition** after robbing a bank   a. elation   b. repentance
   c. recantation   d. exoneration   e. sequestration
2. **impertinent** behavior   a. polite   b. unreasonable   c. rude
   d. ordinary   e. playful
3. **tenacious** pursuit of a goal   a. bovine   b. capricious   c. earnest
   d. desultory   e. tortuous
4. **a commodious** office   a. copious   b. mediocre   c. compound
   d. efficacious   e. ample

Circle the letter of the best ANTONYM (the word or phrase most nearly opposite the word in bold-faced type).

5. to **abstain from** voting   a. avoid   b. participate in
   c. recommend   d. discourage   e. subvert
6. **condoning** a misdemeanor   a. approving   b. reporting
   c. averting   d. forgiving   e. condemning
7. a(n) **pertinacious** spirit   a. uninvolved   b. stubborn   c. lively
   d. tenacious   e. yielding
8. familiar **colloquialisms**   a. odes   b. songs   c. incantations
   d. conversations   e. formal speech

EXERCISE 5B   Circle the letter of the sentence in which the word in bold-faced type is used incorrectly.

1. a. The poster was so large that no amount of tape would make it
      coherent to the wall.
   b. The four movements of Beethoven's *Eroica* Symphony **cohere** in
      musical patterns and heroic theme.
   c. Designers of automobiles must understand the structure of each
      part and aim for **coherence** of the whole.
   d. Although quilting from necessity, using unmatched scraps of
      cloth, nineteenth-century women often created works of art,
      coherent in design and gemlike in color.
2. a. Scornful of the dangers of the bullring and **tenacious** throughout
      rigorous training, a number of girls have become celebrated
      toreras, or bullfighters.
   b. After their ship sank, the survivors kept a **tenacious** grip on
      floating debris until the Coast Guard rescued them.
   c. Immigrants to the United States often cling **tenaciously** to their
      native culture.
   d. People enjoy the **tenacity** of holding and petting furry animals.

3. a. Acknowledging lack of information for the vote, two committee members said, "I **abstain**."
    b. Every gardener must **abstain** weeds before they subvert more valuable plants.
    c. **Abstention** from regular exercise is injurious to your health, but **abstinence** from fatty foods is not.
    d. Some people cannot **abstain** from eating chocolate.
4. a. In both the Old and New Testaments, wearing sackcloth and ashes is considered an act of **contrition**.
    b. The decoration committee regretted the **contriteness** of their homecoming float, judged a mediocrity.,
    c. **Contrite** after slaying his children, Hercules performed the Twelve Labors to express his remorse.
    d. In the novel *Crime and Punishment* Raskolnikov commits what he believes is the perfect crime but feels **contrite** when he realizes the great harm he has done.
5. a. The Greek goddess Hera never **condones** impertinence that negates her power.
    b. Insistent demand for attention is more easily **condoned** in a young child than in a teenager.
    c. Although I understand your anxiety, I cannot **condone** plagiarism—your copying someone else's thoughts and presenting them as your own.
    d. As children grow older they are willing to **condone** their teddy bears and other toys to the closet or the attic.
6. a. **Commiserating** with persecuted Jews in the 1940s, citizens of the French town Le Chambon-sur-Lignon united selflessly to conceal refugees.
    b. Elated baseball fans **commiserated** with Nolan Ryan when he set a record by striking out batter number 5,000.
    c. With the Hebrew prayer, the Kaddish, families express their **commiseration** with one another after the death of a relative.
    d. Observing the poverty of workers seeking her husband's medical help, the artist Käthe Kollwitz expressed her **commiseration** in realistic etchings and woodcuts.
7. a. Although the fictional House of the Seven Gables can be called **commodious** in size, its ghostly occupants make it an uncomfortable house to live in.
    b. Taking to the highways in **commodious** house trailers, travelers enjoy conveniences like those at home.
    c. Most people choose friends who are **commodious**, willing to condone their odd notions and irritating habits.
    d. The artist worked in a **commodious** studio that had once been a warehouse.

8. a. When rock fans become too eager for personal contact, their
pertinacity sometimes verges on impertinence.
   b. Robert Frost's poem "Birches" is **pertinacious** to the idea that a
boy once swung on the birch tree now bent with ice.
   c. Linus Pauling was a **pertinacious** exponent of the theory that
regular doses of vitamin C will prevent colds.
   d. **Pertinacity** in her methods of breeding sled dogs and of her own
physical preparedness has made Susan Butcher a repeat winner
of the Iditarod, a race across Alaska.

EXERCISE 5C

The term *colloquial* applies to the language we use in casual speech but
which is grammatically correct and avoids slang. For example, after dining at a friend's house a person might say, (1) "Hey, that was good grub"
(slang); (2) "Thanks for a great meal" (colloquial); or (3) "Thank you
for a splendid dinner" (formal, the latter more likely to be written than
spoken).

The following underlined colloquialisms have a standard English
equivalent among the words that you have learned in Lesson 5. In the
space provided, rewrite the sentence using more formal words for the colloquialisms in italic type.

1. I *really feel sorry for you.*

   _____

2. I hardly ever *hold back* when I'm asked a question in class.

   _____

3. You live in a *pretty big* house.

   _____

4. When you want something badly, you show *the quality of really keeping
at things*, don't you?

   _____

5. Stop making those *sassy* remarks!

   _____

6. How do you make things *fit together* so well?

   _____

7. When you said "bubbler" instead of "drinking fountain," your
everyday speech let me know you are from the Midwest.

   _____ (Write one word in this space.)

LESSON 6

Jungere dextras.
To join right hands (i.e., to shake hands).—VIRGIL

Key Words

adjunct	inept	strait
aptitude	injunction	stringent
astringent	juncture	subjugate
conjugate		

Familiar Words
apt
lariat

APO, APERE, EPI, APTUM <L. "to fasten," "to attach"

1. **aptitude**   (ăp′tə tōōd)
   n. A natural talent or ability; quickness in learning.

   Fulfilling an essential role, Cherokee women for centuries proved their **aptitude** for agriculture, developing ingenious farming methods.

2. **inept**   (ĭn ĕpt′)   [*in* = <L. "not"]
   adj. 1. Without skill.

   So **inept** that he cannot kick a football or fly a kite, Charlie Brown suffers Lucy's perennial contempt.

   2. Inappropriate or out of place; foolish or absurd.

   To say "Hi, there!" upon meeting a dignified official would be **inept**.

   ineptitude, *n.*

Familiar Words
conjunction
join
junction

JUNGO, JUNGERE, JUNXI, JUNCTUM <L. "to join"

Challenge Words
conjoin
enjoin
junta
subjoin
subjunctive

3. **adjunct**   (ăj′ŭngkt)   [*ad* <L. "to," "toward"]
   n. An added part not essential to the whole.

   The coccyx, or "tailbone," an **adjunct** of the spinal column, no longer has a function.

   adjunctive, *adj.*

4. **conjugate**   (kŏn′jə gāt)   [*con = cum* <L. "with"]
    tr. v. To give forms of verbs in a fixed order.

    Conjugate the present tense of the verb "to see" as follows: I see, you see, he sees (singular); we see, you see, they see (plural).

    conjugation, *n.*

5. **injunction**   (ĭn jŭngk′shən)   [*in* <L. "in"]
    n. An authoritative command or order.

    University students in China received an **injunction** against protest marches.

6. **juncture**   (jŭngk′chər)
    n. 1. A serious state of affairs.

    Environmentalists say that at this **juncture** we must protect rain forests around the globe to prevent harmful atmospheric changes.

    2. The condition or point of being joined.

    The Panama Canal has provided the **juncture** of the Atlantic and Pacific Oceans.

7. **subjugate**   (sŭb′jə gāt′)   [*sub* <L. "under"]
    tr. v. To conquer; to dominate completely.

    Soon after the German army **subjugated** Poland in 1939, Britain declared war.

    subjugation, *n.*

STRINGO, STRINGERE, STRINXI, STRICTUM <L. "to draw together tightly," "to tie"

8. **astringent**   (ə strĭn′jənt)   [*a = ad* <L. "to"]
    adj. Harsh; severe.

    Astringent criticism from one political candidate often draws an equally biting response from an opponent.

    n. A substance that tightens tissues. (In medicine, a substance constricting living tissue.)

    If you nick yourself, apply an **astringent** to stop the bleeding.

    astringency, *n.*

Familiar Words
strict
prestige
restrict
restriction

<table>
<tr><td>

Challenge Words
constrain
constraint
restrictive
stricture

</td></tr>
</table>

9. **strait**   (strāt)
   n. 1. A narrow passage of water connecting two large bodies of water.

   The **Strait** of Gibraltar links the Atlantic Ocean and the Mediterranean Sea.

   2. (usually plural) A difficulty or bad position.

   During the Depression of the 1930s, many people were in economic **straits**.

10. **stringent**   (strĭn′jənt)
    adj. 1. Severe; constricted; tight.

    Members of the Constitutional Convention met under **stringent** rules of secrecy lest rumor leak out and subvert their effort.

    2. Pertaining to scarcity of money.

    Because of **stringent** budget cuts, some schools could no longer finance programs in music and art.

    stringency, *n.*; **stringently**, *adv.*

EXERCISE 6A

Circle the letter of the best SYNONYM (the word or phrase most nearly the same as the word in bold-faced type).

1. a **juncture** in the family's welfare   a. confusion   b. crisis
   c. separation   d. puncture   e. healing
2. a presidential **injunction**   a. award   b. suggestion   c. command
   d. committee   e. issue
3. **aptitude** in science   a. experience   b. fame   c. opinion
   d. failure   e. talent
4. to **subjugate** a people   a. exonerate   b. offend   c. mollify
   d. fight   e. conquer
5. an expert in **conjugation**   a. chairing meetings   b. cheerleading
   c. marriage counseling   d. ordering verb forms   e. manufacturing
   bottles
6. a(n) **adjunct** to the campsite   a. benefit   b. route   c. recent
   addition   d. essential addition   e. nonessential addition

Circle the letter of the best ANTONYM (the word or phrase most nearly opposite the word in bold-faced type).

7. a **stringent** rule   a. perennial   b. severe   c. relaxed   d. perverse   e. useful

8. a songwriter's **astringent** parody   a. soothing   b. asinine   c. omniscient   d. salient   e. abject

9. sudden academic **straits**   a. difficulties   b. confusion   c. channels   d. successes   e. rigors

10. a(n) **inept** renegade   a. artless   b. clever   c. clumsy   d. capricious   e. devious

EXERCISE 6B

Circle the letter of the sentence in which the word in bold-faced type is used incorrectly.

1. a. The city council placed an **injunction** against new buildings of more than three stories.
   b. My parents' **injunction** was "Be home by midnight."
   c. She sent out fifteen **injunctions** to her birthday party.
   d. Some Muslim women obey the **injunction** to wear a *chador*, a garment covering all but the face and hands.

2. a. By urging independence from Great Britain, Mahatma Gandhi brought on a sharp **juncture** in Indian affairs.
   b. We agreed to meet at the **juncture** of three major highways.
   c. At **junctures**, when the world's supply of petroleum appears to dwindle, nuclear energy becomes a crucial issue.
   d. Although we had studied the map carefully, we were surprised to find the two roads **juncturing**.

3. a. After William the Conqueror **subjugated** the Anglo-Saxons in 1066, French became the official language in England.
   b. **Subjugating** our bad habits is a life-long task.
   c. Distinguished actresses like Katharine Cornell and Helen Hayes are able to **subjugate** their personalities in order to play a variety of characters unlike themselves.
   d. English trifle is a dessert that **subjugates** layers of cake and fruit under whipped cream.

4. a. The family's financial **straits** forced a move to a smaller house.
   b. Ships carrying oil passed from the Persian Gulf through the **Strait** of Hormuz to the Gulf of Oman.
   c. **Strait** talk is better than beating around the bush.
   d. When a company shuts down, the entire town where it is located can be thrown into dire **straits**.

5. a. For a small wound, such as a pierced ear, peroxide is a recommended **astringent**, with less sting than rubbing alcohol.
   b. Comedians like Lily Tomlin and Woody Allen are sometimes **astringent** in the characters they create but are nevertheless sympathetic to most human weakness.
   c. Sailors need to know how to tie **astringent** knots.
   d. Students complained about the **astringency** of the punishment for excessive tardiness: a week of suspension.

EXERCISE 6C   Fill in each blank with the most appropriate word from Lesson 6. Use a word or any of its forms only once.

1. A(n) _____ to the flight of the satellite *Voyager 2* past Neptune has been the discovery of that planet's eight moons, previously thought to be only two.

2. Comedy teams like Abbott and Costello and Laurel and Hardy make us laugh because they are so _____ in handling objects and so ready to misunderstand one another.

3. Having not only a(n) _____ for but also a love of flying, Amelia Earhart proved that women could play an important role in aviation.

4. When you _____ the verb *swim* through six tenses in the third person plural, you supply the following: they swim, they swam, they will swim, they have swum, they had swum, and they will have swum.

5. Although adolescents often complain that parental rules about dating are too _____, they usually grow to appreciate the limitations.

REVIEW EXERCISES FOR LESSONS 5 AND 6

1   Matching: On the line at the left, write the letter of the word or phrase
that most accurately defines the word in the left-hand column.

_____	**1.** tenacity	A.	an uncrucial addition
_____	**2.** strait	B.	serious matters
_____	**3.** subjugation	C.	severity
_____	**4.** contrition	D.	shared sorrow
_____	**5.** coherence	E.	avoidance
_____	**6.** colloquialism	F.	skin tightener
_____	**7.** stringency	G.	sincere repentance
_____	**8.** commiseration	H.	order of verb forms
_____	**9.** injunction	I.	clumsiness
_____	**10.** ineptitude	J.	everyday speech
_____	**11.** junctures	K.	persistence
_____	**12.** aptitude	L.	command
_____	**13.** astringent	M.	narrow water passage
_____	**14.** abstention	N.	sticking together
_____	**15.** conjugation	O.	domination
_____	**16.** adjunct	P.	natural ability

2   Fill in the blank or circle the letter of the best answer.

1. colloquial : stiffly formal speech : :
    a. stringent : tight control
    b. conjugated : orderly formation of verbs
    c. inept : awkward movement
    d. commodious : cramped living quarters
    e. subjugated : freedom
2. *stringere* : to tie : : *tenere* : _____
3. Which of the following English words does *not* contain a Latin root
    or prefix meaning "to join"?
    a. conjugate   b. juncture   c. aptitude   d. subjugate   e. adjunct

3 Writing or Discussion Activities

1. Many situations can make a person feel *contrite*. Write a brief letter of apology from yourself or someone else giving details to show *contrition* in a particular situation, imaginary or real. Make clear the reasons for the strong feelings.

2. The word *condone* moves in the opposite direction from *contrite*: a person observes a fault in someone else but does not let it interfere with the relationship. Write a brief letter to assure someone that you *condone* an action that another person might not view so sympathetically. Include a brief description of the action or offense and give reasons for supporting the person involved.

3. Answer one of these three questions in a short paragraph, explaining why you said *yes* or *no*.
   a. Are you a *pertinacious* person?
   b. Do you have a particular *aptitude*?
   c. Have you been in a situation to *commiserate* with someone?

LESSONS 7 AND 8

Separation

LESSON 7

Ab ovo usque ad mala.
From eggs to apples.*—HORACE

Key Words		
abhor	abstemious	discreet
abound	ascertain	infraction
abrasive	discern	infringe
abscond		suffrage

Familiar Words
aberration
abject
abnormal
abolish
abomination
abrupt
absent
absolute
absorb

AB <L. "away from"

1. **abrasive**   (ə brā′sĭv)   [*radere* <L. "to scrape"]
   adj. Harsh; rough.

   The **abrasive** texture of a sandpaper smooths the surface of wood.

   abrade, *v.*; **abrasion**, *n.*; **abrasively**, *adv.*

---

*Eggs and apples represent the first and last courses of a Roman meal; in modern terms, from soup to nuts.

2. **abound** (ə bound′) [*unda* <L. "wave"]
intr. v. 1. To exist in great quantities or numbers.

Although in the nineteenth century buffalo herds **abounded** on the Great Plains, very few are roaming the range today.

2. To be fully supplied or filled.

Despite the heroine's adversities, the musical *Annie* **abounds** in energy and optimism.

abundance, *n.*; **abundantly**, *adv.*

3. **abscond** (ăb skŏnd)
[*condere* <L. "to put together," "to form"]
intr. v. To leave quickly and secretly and hide oneself.

Although grateful for the Bishop's kindness, Jean Valijean nevertheless **absconds** with his host's silverware.

4. **abhor** (ăb hôr′) [*horrere* <L. "to shudder"]
tr. v. To detest thoroughly.

To show that they **abhor** the slaughter of whales, the protesters blocked the path of whaling vessels.

abhorrence, *n.*; **abhorrent**, *adj.*

5. **abstemious** (ăb stē′mē əs)
[*temetus* <L. "liquor," "mead," "wine"]
adj. Sparing or moderate, especially in eating and drinking.

On a long sea voyage in a small craft with limited food supplies, the crew must be **abstemious**.

abstemiously, *adv.*; **abstemiousness**, *n.*

CERNO, CERNERE, CREVI, CRETUM <L. "to separate," "to sift," "to decide"

6. **discreet** (dĭs krēt′) [*dis* <L. "apart"]
adj. Showing tact, respect, and restraint in speech or behavior.

Few of Shakespeare's characters are more gentle and **discreet** than Desdemona, who suffers false accusations with patience.

Challenge Words
discrete
dictionary

discreetly, *adv.*; **discreetness**, *n.*; **discretion**, *n.*
Antonym: **indiscreet**.

NOTA BENE: *Discrete* looks almost the same as *discreet* but has *two* different meanings: "separate from others" and "having separate parts," as in "The short stories in the Edgar Allen Poe collection are *discrete* literary works."

7. **ascertain** (ăs´ər tān´)   [*ad* <L. "to"]
tr. v. To find out something for certain.

The handwriting expert **ascertained** that a diary supposedly written by Hitler was a forgery.

ascertainable, *adj.*

8. **discern** (dĭ sûrn´, dĭ zûrn´)   [*dis* <L. "apart"]
tr. v. To perceive; to detect differences.

Through the sophisticated telescope at Palomar Observatory, astronomers can **discern** stars millions of light years away.

discerning, *adj.*; **discernible**, *adj.*; **discernment**, *n.*

FRANGO, FRANGERE, FREGI, FRACTUM <L. "to break"

Familiar Words
fraction
fracture
fragile
fragment

9. **infraction** (ĭn frăk´shən)   [*in* <L. "in"]
n. A violation, especially of a law.

Crossing against a red light is a more serious **infraction** for a driver than for a pedestrian.

infarct, *v.*

Challenge Words
fracas
fractious
frangible

10. **infringe** (ĭn frĭnj´)   [*in* <L. intensifier]
intr. v. To go beyond set limits (used with *on* or *upon*).

As computers store more and more personal data, citizens may worry that they **infringe** upon an individual's privacy.

infringement, *n.*

11. **suffrage** (sŭf´rĭj)   [*suf* = *sub* <L. "under." (In Roman times a broken piece of poetry was used to signify a vote.)]
n. The right to vote, or a vote itself.

In 1920 Congress amended the Constitution to grant **suffrage** to women.

suffragist, *n.*

NOTA BENE: *Suffragette* is also a related word but applies chiefly to the women's suffrage movement in Great Britain.

NOTA BENE: The Greek word for "break" is *klan*; an *iconoclast* is one who breaks an *icon* or "image," one who overthrows or destroys established traditions or attitudes. Other forms of the word are the adjective *iconoclastic* and the noun *iconoclasm.*

EXERCISE 7A

Circle the letter of the best SYNONYM (the word or phrase most nearly the same as the word in bold-faced type).

1. **abstemious** at the dinner table   a. gluttonous   b. moderate
   c. fussy   d. talkative   e. tenacious
2. to **infringe** upon others' property   a. intrude   b. expound
   c. mediate   d. rely   e. caper
3. to **abscond** with the prize money   a. return   b. defer   c. exult
   d. abstain   e. flee
4. **abounding** good will   a. cheering   b. diminishing   c. endless
   d. occasional   e. deferring

Circle the letter of the best ANTONYM (the word or phrase most nearly opposite the word in bold-faced type).

5. **abrasive** in conducting business   a. rude   b. inept   c. courteous
   d. rough   e. enterprising
6. **abhorrence** of cruelty   a. hatred   b. love   c. subjugation
   d. negation   e. discernment
7. a(n) **discreet** reply   a. percussive   b. mild   c. discerning
   d. contrite   e. abrasive
8. to **ascertain** the earth's circumference   a. calculate   b. infer
   c. be ignorant of   d. distort   e. describe

EXERCISE 7B

Circle the letter of the sentence in which the word in bold-faced type is used incorrectly.

1. a. An admirer of the work of Mary Cassatt **discerned** a fake listed as one of her impressionistic paintings at the auction.
   b. Columbus **discerned** American in 1492.
   c. Sherlock Holmes's **discernment** of hidden clues often dazzles his friend Dr. Watson, a qualified doctor but an amateur sleuth.
   d. We sometimes have trouble **discerning** fact from fiction.

2.   a.   Songs, folk plays, riddles, and games **abounding** in Spanish folklore have kept the Spanish language alive in the American Southwest.
   b.   Passenger pigeons, which **abounded** in the United States a century ago, are now extinct.
   c.   Varieties of tempting pastries **abounded** in the bakery window.
   d.   The Gobi Desert **abounds** with water.

3.   a.   Ugly, smelly decay of plants and animals may seem an **abhorrence**, but it is in fact nature's efficacious process of recycling and revival.
   b.   The philosopher Spinoza observed, "Nature **abhors** a vacuum."
   c.   We made some really **abhorring** costumes for the Halloween party.
   d.   Psychologists tell us that people living in rooms painted purple develop an **abhorrence** of that color.

4.   a.   Successive dry summers and scanty harvests in 1798 and 1799 caused severe **suffrage** for Scottish farmers.
   b.   Strife in South Africa has centered around the denial of **suffrage** to the nonwhite population.
   c.   Until amended in 1920, the U.S. Constitution granted **suffrage** only to males.
   d.   British "**suffragettes**" went on hunger strikes in prison to shame the government into letting women vote.

5.   a.   The woman known as Typhoid Mary committed numerous **infractions** of health laws by knowingly spreading typhoid fever germs while employed as a cook.
   b.   If we look carefully we can see a small **infraction** in this heirloom vase.
   c.   Hitchhiking on freeways is an **infraction** of state law.
   d.   After meeting the Queen of Hearts in Wonderland, Alice learns that the smallest **infraction** sets up the shout, "Off with her [or his] head!"

6.   a.   An **abrasive** brush will clean and polish metal pans.
   b.   In Rome air pollution has so **abraded** bronze statues that some are permanently damaged.
   c.   Talk show hosts intrigue television audiences with clever retorts but may offend people when they become **abrasive**.
   d.   The students realized too late that they had committed an **abrasion** of judgment by crashing the party.

7.   a.   Even when handcuffed and locked in a capsule submerged in water, Harry Houdini could **ascertain** an escape.
   b.   Scientists have **ascertained** that fear of punishment retards learning.
   c.   With television coverage of government sessions, the public can **ascertain** the effectiveness of elected officials.
   d.   Opinion polls on every subject from food to politics attempt to **ascertain** our preferences, which, however, shift from day to day.

EXERCISE 7C   Fill in each blank with the most appropriate word from Lesson 7. Use a word or any of its forms only once.

1. After persuading gullible victims to hand over their life savings, the

   trickster _____ed.

2. Uninvited sales pitches over the telephone _____ upon our time and privacy.

3. Although the confidante of many friends, she was always

   _____, never revealing any secrets.

4. Hosts who have prepared a grand dinner do not want their guests

   to be _____.

5. Driving above the speed limit is a(n) _____ which, if it goes on file, may increase the cost of car insurance.

6. Although American citizens are eligible to vote at age eighteen, a sizeable number of them do not exercise their right of

   _____.

7. Only when the fog lifted could we begin to _____ the outlines of New York's skyscrapers.

LESSON 8

Toto caelo.
(Separated) by the whole heavens (diametrically opposite).

Key Words		
absolve	concise	resolve
analyze	herbicide	superfluous
catalyst	precise	superlative
	resolute	

Familiar Words
superabundant
superficial
superior
superman
supermarket
supernatural
superstar
superstition
supervise
supreme

SUPER <L. "above"

1. **superlative**   (soo pûr′lə tĭv)   [*latum* <L. "carried"]
   adj. The highest; above the rest.

   Superlative builders of irrigation systems, the Pueblo peoples had much to teach seventeenth-century colonists in New Mexico.

   NOTA BENE: *Superlative* is also a grammatical term used to describe the third form in a series of adjectives: *tall* (positive); *taller* (comparative); *tallest* (superlative).

2. **superfluous** (soo pûr′floo əs)
[*fluere* <L. "to flow"]
adj. Beyond what is required; extra.

Because it no longer serves a purpose, the appendix has become **superfluous** in human beings.

superfluity, *n.*; **superfluously**, *adv.*

CAEDO, CAEDERE, CECIDI, CAESUM <L. "to cut"

3. **concise** (kən sīs′) [*con = cum* <L. "with"]
adj. Saying or writing much in few words.

"Experience teaches" is a **concise** way to say that what happens in our daily lives guides us in subsequent actions.

concisely, *adv.*; **conciseness**, *n.*

4. **herbicide** (hûr′bĭ sīd) [*herba* <L. "grass," "plants with stems"]
n. A substance for killing plants, especially weeds.

The **herbicide** known as Agent Orange was used in Vietnam to kill vegetation.

herbicidal, *adj.*

5. **precise** (prĭ sīs′) [*pre = prae* <L. "before," "in front of"]
adj. Clearly expressed; exact; accurate in every detail.

Sending a satellite to photograph the planet Neptune millions of miles from Earth requires **precise** calculations.

precisely, *adv.*; **precision**, *n.*
Antonym: **imprecise**

NOTA BENE: Another word that means "to cut" or "to split" is the Greek word *skhizein*, which gives us the English word *schism* (sĭz′m, skĭz′m), "a separation or division into factions," as in "A *schism* exists between Democrats and Republicans." Another derivative from *skhizein* is the term *schizophrenia*, "a mental disturbance that separates one from reality."

LUEIN <G. "to loosen," "to untie"
LUTOS <G. "capable of being untied"

6. **analyze** (ăn′ə līz) [*ana* <G. "on," "up"]
tr. v. To look at something carefully by attention to its parts.

When doctors analyze the nature of cells, they find ways to fight disease.

> **Challenge Words**
> dialysis
> proselytize

analysis (plural **analyses**), *n.*; **analytical**, adj.

7. **catalyst**   (kăt′əl ĭst)   [*cata* <G. "down from"]
n. A force or person causing action, especially without being involved or changed by the consequences.

Mahatma Gandhi served as the **catalyst** for the nonviolent political change adopted by Martin Luther King, Jr.

NOTA BENE: In chemistry, a *catalyst* is a substance that causes or accelerates change but remains unaffected itself.

catalysis, *n.*; **catalytic**, *adj.*; **catalytically**, *adv.*; **catalyze**, *v.*

SOLVO, SOLVERE, SOLVI, SOLUTUM <L. "to loosen," "to untie"

> **Familiar Words**
> absolute
> dissolve
> soluble
> solution
> solve

8. **absolve**   (äb zôlv′, ăb sŏlv′)   [*ab* <L. "away from"}
tr. v. To relieve of blame or obligation; to pardon a sin.

Although we were sequestered with the culprits for questioning, our innocence **absolved** us from punishment.

absolution, *n.*; **absolved**, *adj.*.

> **Challenge Words**
> dissolution
> resoluble

9. **resolute**   (rĕz′ə lo͞ot)   [*re* <L. "back," "again"]
adj. Determined; unshakable.

Resolute even though paralyzed and in a wheelchair, Ruth Rosenbaum has won Olympic medals in slalom, shot put, discus, and javelin.

resolutely, *adv.*; **resolution**, *n.*
Antonym: **irresolute**

10. **resolve**   (rĭ zŏlv′)   [*re* <L. "back," "again"]
tr. v. 1. To make a firm decision about.

She **resolved** to run five miles every morning.

NOTA BENE: In formal debate, issues appear in the following form: *Resolved*: that the social committee will stay within its budget.

2. To find a solution.

The mediator **resolved** the conflict.

resolution, *n.*; **resolved**, *adj.*

EXERCISE 8A   Circle the letter of the best SYNONYM (the word or phrase most nearly the same as the word in bold-faced type).

   1. **resolute** in completing her legal studies a. capricious b. perverse
      c. perservering d. erratic e. concise
   2. **precision** in speaking a. ineptitude b. exactness c. volubility
      d. deception e. haste
   3. a(n) **catalyst** for change a. precursor b. reason c. procedure
      d. force e. adjunct
   4. **analysis** of the crime a. investigation b. catalyst c. premonition
      d. depiction e. evidence
   5. an efficacious **herbicide** a. insect repellent b. grass seed
      c. plant food d. fungus e. weed killer

Circle the letter of the best ANTONYM (the word or phrase most nearly opposite the word in bold-faced type).

   6. expectation of **absolution** a. exoneration b. freedom
      c. blame d. infringement e. adversity
   7. **superfluity** of goods a. excess b. sufficiency c. transitoriness
      d. worthlessness e. inadequacy
   8. to **resolve** a conflict a. inflame b. conclude c. reconsider
      d. mediate e. resume
   9. **superlative** performances a. contorted b. extraneous
      c. mediocre d. exorbitant e. superior
  10. **concise** statements a. voluble b. brief c. expository
      d. summary e. abrasive

EXERCISE 8B   Circle the letter of the sentence in which the word in bold-faced type is used incorrectly.

   1. a. When the electricity fails, students may feel **absolved** from
         completing their homework.
      b. Martin Luther so abhorred the sale of "indulgences," certificates
         that **absolved** sins with money, that he made a public protest
         against church policy.
      c. The balloon slowly **absolved** from its ropes and floated away.
      d. People sometimes hope that a winning lottery ticket will **absolve**
         them from debts.
   2. a. Following the uproar in 1939 over her being barred from singing
         at Constitution Hall, Marian Anderson served as a **catalyst** for
         African-American female singers.
      b. Water often acts as a **catalytic** agent.

    c. The American Revolution served as a **catalyst** for French revolutionists.

    d. My dog is **catalytic**; he is terrified of felines.

3. a. **Analysis** of well water near the manufacturing plant showed the presence of toxic material.

    b. When **analyzed,** her handwriting revealed that she is neat and discreet.

    c. Literary **analysis** explains ideas, gives examples, and generalizes about the author's main point.

    d. Scientists were asked to **analyses** the gases permeating the air around the volcano.

4. a. Mexican *curanderos,* or folk doctors, acquire a **precise** knowledge of medicinal herbs, roots, and wild flowers having curative powers.

    b. Only through years of practice do the great ballerinas develop the **precision** necessary for dancing *Swan Lake* and *Romeo and Juliet.*

    c. Manufacturers act **precisely** when they cut out high fat and calorie content in food products.

    d. The appearance of "Error" on a computer screen jolts the user into giving more **precise** commands.

5. a. According to automobile enthusiasts, the Dusenberg of the 1920s and 1930s remains the **superlative** classic car.

    b. There is only one Eiffel Tower, and it is **superlative**.

    c. Two **superlative** jazz singers, renowned for their vocal flexibility and individual styles, are Ella Fitzgerald and Sarah Vaughan.

    d. Anyone who has watched the tennis champion Martina Navratilova knows her to be a **superlative** player: flexible, controlled, and accurate.

EXERCISE 8C

Fill in each blank with the most appropriate word from Lesson 8. Use a word or any of its forms only once.

1. In a series of victories against Spanish forces, Simon Bolivar was a(n)

    _____ for the drive toward independence of South American countries and is significantly remembered in the name of one of them, Bolivia.

2. Packing for an airplane trip usually forces us to leave

    _____ possessions at home.

3. The Australian pediatrician Helen Caldicott has remained

    _____ in her opposition to nuclear weapons, believing that the human race is gravely endangered.

4. Every ice cream company contends that its product is

    _____.

5. Environmentalists deliver injunctions against harmful pesticides and

_____s.

6. Your _____ directions brought us to your house without a moment of indecision—and in so few words!

REVIEW EXERCISES FOR LESSONS 7 AND 8

1 Fill in the blank or circle the letter of the best answer.

1. *frangere* : to break : : *caedere* : _____
2. *cernere* : to separate : : *solvere* : _____
3. abscond : run and hide : :
   a. ascertain : guess
   b. discern : fail to see differences
   c. resolve : find a solution
   d. infringe : respect boundaries
   e. abhor : maintain tolerance
4. abstemious : moderation : :
   a. resolute : indecision
   b. abhorrent : adoration
   c. superfluous : excess
   d. discreet : disrespect
   e. concise : superfluity
5. Which of these English words does *not* have "loosen" or "untie" in its Latin root?
   a. analysis b. paralyze c. resolve d. abstemious e. absolution
6. Which of these English words does *not* contain a root meaning "separate" or "break"?
   a. infraction   b. discern   c. abound   d. suffrage   e. discreet

2 Writing or Discussion Activities

1. Imagine yourself on a camping trip. Use at least four of the following words in a brief paragraph describing people and situations that you are enjoying and that make you feel positive about them. Give concrete details so that your reader can picture the people and the scene.

abound	concise	discreet	absolve
abstemious	discern	resolve	catalyst

2. On the same camping trip you meet people who stimulate unpleasantness or conflict. Use two of the following words in a brief paragraph. Describe a specific incident to show the words in action.

abscond   infraction   superfluous
abrasive   resolve

3. Which one of the words or phrases in the following list best describes you or expresses something that you are not? Write a sentence using your word and giving specific details to support your choice of word.

discreet   abounding in energy (or some other quality)
infringing   abstemious
analytical   concise
catalytic   discerning

PART TWO

Responding

Sight

Directions

1. Determine how the Latin or Greek root is related in meaning and spelling to each defined—KEY—word that follows it.
2. Learn the pronunciation and definition(s) of each KEY word, and notice how the words are used in sentences.
3. Practice using the varied forms of KEY words.
4. Build your knowledge with all the information given: Latin mottoes, Familiar Words, Challenge Words, and Nota Bene references.
5. Complete the exercises.

LESSON 9

Veni, vidi, vici.
I came, I saw, I conquered.—JULIUS CAESAR

Key Words		
improvise	refute	repose
ostensible	reiterate	reticent
ostentatious	repartee	visionary
	repertoire	

Familiar Words
react
recant
recede
recur
regress
reject
remember
reply
repress
repulse
require
respect
restrict
reverse
revise
revolve

Challenge Words
rebate
rebuff
rebuke
recapitulate
recriminate
redress
redundant
reincarnation
remit
repast
repercussion
replicate
reprehend
reprisal
reprobate
reprove
repudiate
rescind

RE <L. "back," "again"

1. refute (rĭ fyo͞ot′) [*futare* <L. *refutare*, "to drive back"]
tr. v. To prove a statement or person to be incorrect; to disprove.

The women's marathon in the Olympics has **refuted** former claims that women are physically incapable of running long distances.

refutability, *n*.; **refutable**, *adj*.; **refutably**, *adv*.; **refuter**, *n*.; **refutation**, *n*.

2. reiterate (rē ĭt′ə rāt) [*iterum* <L. "again"]
tr. v. To say over again.

Our coach **reiterated** her familiar advice: Don't exhaust yourself in the first quarter.

reiteration, *n*.; **reiterative**, *adj*.

3. repartee (rĕp′ər tē′, rĕp′ər tā′, rĕp′är tā′)
[*partire* <L. "to part"]
n. 1. A quick, witty reply.

Their insulting **repartee** makes Beatrice and Benedick in *Much Ado About Nothing* one of Shakespeare's favorite couples.

2. Conversation characterized by such remarks.

Although gifted at small talk and **repartee**, he seems incapable of serious discussion.

NOTA BENE: Many words have a similar *detonation*, or dictionary definition, but differ in their *connotation*, the ideas a word suggests beyond its definition. For example, *answer* and *reply* are neutral in connotation. On the other hand, while both *repartee* and *retort* can be defined as "a witty reply," they differ in their connotation. Someone might compliment you by saying, "You are well known for your repartee," meaning you make witty "comebacks" in conversation. You might be less pleased to hear "You are well known for your retorts," for you are being told that your replies in argument are sharp and often turn an opponent's words against him or her.

4. repertoire (rĕp′ər twär) Also *repertory*. [*parire* <L. "to produce"]
n. 1. The stock of plays, stories, songs, or other pieces that a player or company is prepared to perform.

A march by John Philip Sousa is part of almost every school band's **repertoire**.

2. The skills or accomplishments of a particular person or group.

Most chefs have a recipe for chocolate mousse in their **repertoires**.

5. **repose** (rĕ pōz´)
[*pose* = *positum* <L. *reponere*, "to rest"]
n. A rest; a peaceful state.

Because a hummingbird's wings move so rapidly in flight, the markings on its wings can be observed only when the bird is in **repose**.

tr. v. To place trust in or expectations on something.

In *The Grapes of Wrath* the Joad family leaves its Oklahoma dust bowl farm and **reposes** its hopes on new opportunities to be found in California.

intr. v. To rest.

During the middle of the day, many people in the tropics take a siesta, a time to **repose** until the heat dies down.

reposal, *n.*; **reposeful**, *adj.*; **reposer**, *n.*

6. **reticent** (rĕt´ə sənt) [*tacere* <L. "to be silent"]
adj. Of a silent nature; reserved in manner.

Although habitually **reticent**, he spoke out eloquently against injustice.

reticence, *n.*; **reticently**, *adv.*

OSTENDO, OSTENDERE, OSTENDI, OSTENSUM
<L. "to exhibit"

7. **ostensible** (ŏ stĕn´sə bəl)
adj. Pretended; given as an excuse, to conceal the real reason.

Although her **ostensible** purpose at the courthouse was to meet a client, she really came to pick up information.

ostensibly, *adv.*

8. **ostentatious** (ŏs´tĕn tā´shəs)
adj. Showy; intended to impress people.

They had an **ostentatious** wedding reception with a thousand guests and a ten-foot-high cake.

ostentation, *n.*; **ostentatiously**, *adv.*

Familiar Words
advise
envision
interview
invisible
preview
provide
review
revision
supervise
survey
television
view
vision

Challenge Words
belvedere
clairvoyant
invidious
visa

VIDEO, VIDERE, VIDI, VISUM <L. "to see"

9. **improvise**   (ĭm′prə vīz)   [*in* <L. "not"]
   tr. v. 1. To make up something without preparation.

   Surprised by the nomination, she had to **improvise** her acceptance speech.

   2. To make or provide from materials on hand.

   The shipwrecked crew **improvised** a boat from barrel staves.

   improvisation, *n.*; **improvisational**, *adj.*; **improvised**, *adj.*;
   improvisatory, *adj.*

10. **visionary**   (vĭzh′ən ĕr´ē)
    adj. 1. Existing only in imagination; fanciful; not practical.

    The Jamestown settlers were long on **visionary** schemes but short on funds and common sense.

    2. Characterized by vision or forethought.

    Ida B. Wells's **visionary** goal was equal justice for Americans of all races.

EXERCISE 9A

Circle the letter of the best SYNONYM (the word or phrase most nearly the same as the word in bold-faced type).

1. to **reiterate** instructions   a. mediate on   b. confuse   c. explain
   d. repeat   e. revise
2. their **ostensible** destination   a. pretended   b. intended   c. former
   d. discreet   e. unreachable
3. to seek **repose**   a. improvement   b. revenge   c. tranquility
   d. refutation   e. relocation

Circle the letter of the best ANTONYM (the word or phrase most nearly opposite the word in bold-faced type).

4. overcome your **reticence**   a. weakness   b. shyness   c. talkativeness
   d. silliness   e. elation
5. a(n) **ostentatious** outfit   a. expensive   b. understated
   c. obsequious   d. monstrous   e. becoming
6. enact **visionary** legislation   a. forward-looking   b. improvised
   c. foolish   d. antiquated   e. extravagant
7. claims difficult to **refute**   a. repeat   b. remember   c. prove correct
   d. disbelieve   e. keep watch on

EXERCISE 9B   Circle the letter of the sentence in which the word in bold-faced type is used incorrectly.

1. a. Although a political **visionary**, Thomas Jefferson was also an efficient farmer and businessperson.
   b. Such **visionary** plans feed the imagination but not the belly.
   c. Elaborate **visionary** effects turned our gym into a tropical jungle for the junior prom.
   d. They are a great architectural team: he conceives the **visionary** designs and she interprets them in concrete and steel.

2. a. **Improvised** dances are often as exciting as those carefully choreographed and rehearsed.
   b. We worked all fall to **improvise** new basketball plays for the winter season.
   c. Robinson Crusoe **improvised** an umbrella from banana leaves.
   d. In drama class we made up **improvisational** skits based on phrases we drew from a hat.

3. a. Although I told every joke in my **repertoire**, that audience wouldn't even smile.
   b. The Danish philosopher Sören Kierkegaard led a life of such **repertoire** that people claimed they could set their watches by his daily routine.
   c. The dance band's **repertoire** includes both Brazilian sambas and rock and roll tunes from the fifties.
   d. Our company's **repertoire** is out of date; we need to add some contemporary plays next season.

4. a. In seventeenth-century comedy most of the humor arises from **repartee** among fashionable men and women.
   b. Poland has been subjected to repeated **repartee**, with Germany, Austria, and Russia claiming large areas for themselves.
   c. Among her literary friends at the Algonquin Round Table, Dorothy Parker was more admired for her **repartee** than for her verse.
   d. Although talk show hosts hope to stimulate **repartee** among their guests, their conversations are usually question-and-answer interviews.

5. a. Although Granny seems cheerful and lively, her face in **repose** reveals worry and fatigue.
   b. Rather than **repose** so much faith in the opinions of others, try to make decisions for yourself.
   c. **Repose** that cookie right were you found it! Lunch is almost ready.
   d. Before his funeral John F. Kennedy's **reposed** in the Capitol rotunda.

6. a. Ignoring many scientific **refutations** of astrology, thousands of people read their horoscopes daily.
   b. As the population increases, space for wildlife is steadily **refuted**.
   c. Cicero, the Roman orator, recommended that a speaker first **refute** his opponent's arguments before advancing his own.
   d. Despite her **refuters**, Anastasia continued to assert that she was the only surviving child of Czar Nicholas.
7. a. Although **ostensibly** the Prince of Wales, the boy in the velvet robes was, in fact, Tom Canty, a pauper with whom the true prince had traded places.
   b. Their **ostensible** string quartet was the cover for a smuggling ring.
   c. **Ostensibly** he came to help, but I know he really came to gossip.
   d. An inch of lace was **ostensible** at her hemline.

EXERCISE 9C   Fill in each blank with the most appropriate word from Lesson 9. Use a word or any of its forms only once.

1. Rather than making _____ donations that get their name in headlines, the family prefers to make anonymous contributions to charity.
2. In many Islamic cultures students learn the Koran by

   _____, repeating passages over and over until memorized.
3. Although she engaged in easy repartee on most subjects, about her

   family life she remained _____.
4. Rosa Parks, whose refusal to sit in the back of the bus was one of the triggers of the civil rights movement in the 1960s, acted not because

   of _____ motives but because of fatigue after a long day's work.
5. Too poor after the Civil War to afford to buy fabric, Scarlett O'Hara

   _____d a new dress out of the green velvet parlor curtains.
6. The _____ of folk singer Joan Baez includes songs in both Spanish and English.

LESSON 10

Vigilate et orate.
Watch and pray.—Matthew 26:41

Key Words

auspicious	specimen	surveillance
introspection	specter	vigil
retrospect	spectrum	vigilant
	speculate	

Familiar Words
aspect
conspicuous
despise
expect
inspect
perspective
prospect
species
specific
spectacle
respect

Challenge Word
prospectus

SPECTO, SPECTARE, SPECTAVI, SPECTATUM
<L. "to look at"

1. **auspicious** (ô spĭsh′əs) [*auspicium* <L. "foretelling the future by bird signs"]
   adj. Showing signs that promise success.

   The sunny morning was an **auspicious** beginning for our class picnic.

   auspiciously, *adv.*

2. **introspection** (ĭn′trə spĕk′shən) [*intro* <L. "within," "inward"]
   adj. Examination of one's own thoughts and feelings.

   Experience may help us to understand others, but without **introspection** we will never understand our own motives.

   introspective, *adj.*; **introspectively**, *adv.*

3. **retrospect** (rĕt′rə spĕkt′) [*retro* <L. "backward"]
   n. A survey of past times or events.

   In **retrospect** I wish I had chosen an instrument like the flute when I joined the band rather than this heavy, awkward tuba.

   retrospection, *n.*; **retrospection**, *adj.*

4. **specimen** (spĕs′ə mən)
   n. A single thing that is taken as an example of a whole category.

   The *Apollo* astronauts gathered **specimens** of rock to determine the chemical composition of the moon.

5. **specter**   (spĕk′tər)
   n. 1. A ghost.

   Local legend claims that the **specter** of a jilted lover haunts the chapel.

   2. A haunting fear of future trouble.

   After hail destroyed the corn crop, the **specter** of famine loomed over the village.

   spectral, *adj.*

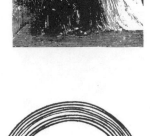

6. **spectrum**   (spĕk′trəm);   (plural **spectra**, **spectrums**)
   n. 1. The distribution of characteristics of a physical system, especially bands of colors seen as a rainbow or bands of differing sound waves.

   Light refracted through a crystal shows all the colors of the **spectrum**.

   2. A wide range of related qualities or ideas.

   Congress represents a wide **spectrum** of opinion.

7. **speculate**   (spĕk′yə lāt)
   intr. v. 1. To form opinions without definite knowledge or evidence.

   Human beings have long **speculated** about life on other planets.

   2. To buy or sell something to make a profit but with risk of loss.

   She made and then lost a fortune **speculating** on the stock market.

   speculation, *n.*;   **speculative**, *adj.*;   **speculator**, *n.*

VIGILO, VIGILARE, VIGILAVI, VIGILATUM <L. "to watch"

Familiar Word
vigilante

8. **surveillance**   (sər vā′ləns)
   [*sur* <French "over" from *super* <L. "over"]
   n. Supervision or close observation, especially of a suspected person.

   As soon as a candidate for President of the United States is nominated, he or she is immediately placed under Secret Service **surveillance**.

   surveillant, *adj.*

Challenge Word
reveille

9. **vigil**   (vĭj′əl)
   n. A period of staying awake to keep watch or to pray.

Because of her nightly **vigils** at the bedsides of dying soldiers during the Crimean War, the nursing pioneer Florence Nightingale became known as "The Lady with the Lamp."

10. **vigilant**   (vĭj′ə lənt)
    adj. Watchful; on the lookout for danger.

    The **vigilant** red-tailed hawks attacked any intruders that approached their nest.

    vigilance, *n.*; **vigilantly**, *adv.*

EXERCISE 10A   Circle the letter of the best SYNONYM (the word or phrase most nearly the same as the word in bold-faced type).

1. an all-night **vigil**   a. party   b. punishment period   c. wakeful period   d. danger period   e. contention
2. to **speculate on** the election results   a. deny   b. argue about   c. infringe on   d. explain away   e. meditate on
3. to keep under **surveillance**   a. lock and key   b. infraction   c. suspicion   d. an illusion   e. close watch
4. his **introspective** mood   a. shy   b. meditative   c. cheerful   d. irritable   e. visionary

Circle the letter of the best ANTONYM (the word or phrase most nearly opposite the word in bold-faced type).

5. a(n) **auspicious** sign   a. foreboding   b. incautious   c. terrifying   d. illegible   e. introspective
6. the **vigilant** sentry   a. cautious   b. alert   c. unwatchful   d. introverted   e. ghostly
7. her **retrospective** point of view   a. forward-looking   b. modest   c. fearful   d. inward-looking   e. delightful

EXERCISE 10B   Circle the letter of the sentence in which the word in bold-faced type is used incorrectly.

1. a. Light passing through a prism breaks into the **spectrum** of colors.
   b. In Willa Cather's novel *My Ántonia* we find the whole social **spectrum** of American frontier life from wealthy farmers to poor immigrants.
   c. The human ear can register only a narrow **spectrum** sounds.
   d. A **spectrum** helps those with weak eyes to see more clearly.

2. a. People like to **speculate** on traveling through time.
   b. The safest **speculation** is to bury your money in the garden.
   c. Columbus thought his **speculations** about how to reach India were proven correct when he discovered the New World.
   d. Madame C.J. Walker amassed a fortune by **speculating** in cosmetic products and beauty salons.

3. a. You can't **specter** me with your threats.
   b. The **specter** of poverty made the family careful about every penny they spent.
   c. Hamlet encounters the **specter** of his dead father, who urges him to avenge his "murder most foul."
   d. Our December vacation was darkened by the **specter** of January exams.

4. a. The **retrospective** exhibit of Imogen Cunningham's photographs showed her works from the last fifty years.
   b. In **retrospect** for your grandparents, don't argue during their visit.
   c. Seeing your errors is far easier in **retrospect**.
   d. The school yearbook makes a **retrospective** summary of the year's events.

5. a. The doctors tested **specimens** of blood and urine from all contestants for evidence of drugs.
   b. The dog show champion should be a perfect **specimen** of its breed.
   c. By examining the **specimens** of animal tracks around the water hole, the hunters could tell which direction the wounded lion had taken.
   d. **Specimens** of basketry from the Pomo people of California show this craft to have been highly developed.

EXERCISE 10C

Fill in each blank with the most appropriate word from Lesson 10. Use a word or any of its forms only once.

1. Many religions encourage self-knowledge through meditation and

   _____ .

2. Although police had the house under constant _____ , the suspect managed to escape disguised as a Saint Bernard.

3. Every year at the anniversary of their guru's death, disciples kept a

   day-long _____ at the tomb.

4. Because they wish to harm no living things, Buddhist monks walk

   _____ly to avoid stepping on insects.

5. Steffi Graf's talent, training, and record made her a(n)

    _____ contender for the world tennis championship.

6. The botanical garden is trying to obtain at least one _____ of every native American tree.

7. The _____ of nuclear war threatened the late twentieth century.

REVIEW EXERCISES FOR LESSONS 9 AND 10

1

Fill in the blanks or circle the letter of the best answer.

1. *videre* : *ostendere* : :
   a. to look at : to watch
   b. to see : to exhibit
   c. revise : revoke
   d. *spectare* : *vigilare*
   e. to look at : to exhibit
2. improvise : rehearse : :
   a. auspicious : promising
   b. vigilant : watchful
   c. ostentatious : modest
   d. ostensible : obvious
   e. refute : repartee
3. introspection : retrospection : :
   a. impose : repose
   b. inspect : expect
   c. specter : ghost
   d. within : backward
   e. look : see
4. Three familiar words that derive from the root *spectare* are

   _____, _____ , and

   _____.

5. *Re* can mean both _____ and _____.
6. *Advise, invisible, preview,* and *supervise* all derive from the root

   _____ , which means _____.

2 Matching: Seated next to you at a party is someone who could be described by the phrase in the left-hand column. On the line at the left, write the letter of the adjective that expresses the same qualities.

_____ 1. Someone who doesn't reveal a lot about himself or herself

_____ 2. Someone wearing many jewels who talks to you about owning yachts and airplanes

_____ 3. Someone who speaks more often about the past than the future

_____ 4. Someone lost in deep personal thoughts

_____ 5. Someone who keeps a constantly watchful eye on a very active child

_____ 6. Someone who is as pale as a ghost

_____ 7. Someone who tells you about her dreams for the future

A. improvisatory

B. auspicious

C. vigilant

D. retrospective

E. spectral

F. introspective

G. reticent

H. visionary

I. ostentatious

3 Writing or Discussion Activities

1. Write a short dialogue that illustrates *repartee.* Your characters may be real or imaginary.
2. Write sentences using any *two* words from each group.
   a. specter, reticent, ostensible, vigil
   b. repertoire, refute, ostentatious, reticent
3. Describe in a sentence a situation in which you have had to *improvise.* Use *improvise* or one of its related forms in your sentence.
4. Describe in a brief paragraph the clothing, room, or behavior of an *ostentatious* person. Use *ostentatious* or one of its related forms in your paragraph.
5. Describe in a few sentences a setting that would invite *repose* and *introspection.* Use either word in your description.

LESSONS 11 AND 12

The Other Senses

LESSON 11

Ad astra per aspera.
To the stars through difficulties.

Key Words		
ad hoc	evoke	redolent
admonish	olfactory	resonate
advocate	provocative	sonic
assimilate		vociferous

AD <L. "to," "toward"

NOTA BENE: When *ad* comes before roots beginning with certain letters, it changes, as the following examples illustrate:

before *c*	*ac*	*accustom*	before *n*	*an*	*annex*
before *f*	*af*	*affix*	before *q*	*ac*	*acquaintance*
before *g*	*ag*	*aggression*	before *r*	*ar*	*arrest*
before *l*	*al*	*allure*	before *s*	*as*	*associate*

Knowing this rule can help improve your spelling!

Familiar Words
access
accord
account
accrue
addict
adhere
adjective
adjoin
admit
adverb
aggravate
allure
annex
arrest
assail
assist

Challenge Words
accredit
acquiesce
ad lib
ad nauseam
adverse
advocate
aggression
alleviate
alliterate
annul
array

1. **ad hoc**   (ăd hŏk′)   [L. "toward this"]
   adj. For a specific purpose or situation.

   The **ad hoc** campaign committee will disband after the election.

2. **admonish**   (ăd mŏn′ĭsh)
   [*monere* <L. "to advise"]
   tr. v. 1. To scold gently but firmly.

   Our camp counselor **admonished** us
   to quit talking and go to sleep.

   2. To caution; to warn.

   Although **admonished** by the ranger to keep to the trail, the hikers set
   off cross-country and were soon lost.

   admonition, *n.*; **admonitory**, *adj.*

3. **assimilate**   (ə sĭm′ə lāt)   [*simulare* <L. "to stimulate"]
   v. 1. To take in and make a part of the body; to digest.

   The body **assimilates** sugars and carbohydrates rapidly, but proteins
   and fats require longer digestion.

   2. To cause to become similar or part of a whole.

   America's "melting pot" society has **assimilated** cultures from every
   part of the globe.

   assimilation, *n.*; **assimilative**, *adj.*; **assimilator**, *n.*

   NOTA BENE: Although *ad* usually appears in English as a prefix, several phrases retain *ad* as a separate word. Like *ad hoc*, many of these phrases are related to time and money:
   - *ad inifinitum*—"to the point of infinity" or "endlessly."
   - *ad libitum* or its abbreviation *ad lib*—"done freely and without planning" or "off the cuff."
   - *ad nauseam*—"to the point of disgust" or "excessively."
   - *ad valorem*—"in proportion to the value of something."

   Other *ad* phrases relate to rhetoric, the art of public speaking, a skill the Romans considered essential to every educated person. In particular these phrases with *ad* describe certain kinds of good and bad arguments:
   - *ad hominem*—"appealing to personal interests such as a person's prejudices or individual advantage, rather than to reason."
   - *ad rem*—"to the point."

   In most cases these *ad* phrases have been carried over from Latin into English because the Latin phrase is more concise than its English translation.

OLEO, OLERE, OLUI <L. "to smell"

4. **olfactory** (ŏl fǎk′tər ē, ŏl fǎk′trē) [*facere* <L. "to make"]
   adj. Pertaining to the sense of smell.

   Expert perfumers have such a developed **olfactory** sense that they can identify the various scents in a complex fragrance.

   olfaction, *n.*

5. **redolent** (rĕd′ə lənt)
   adj. 1. Smelling strongly.

   After we made lasagna, the kitchen was **redolent** of garlic.

   2. Full of memories.

   My grandparents' attic is **redolent** of my childhood afternoons spent reading there.

   redolence, *n.*; **redolently**, *adv.*

Familiar Words
consonant
resound
sonnet
sound
unison

SONO, SONARE, SONUI, SONITUM <L. "to sound"

6. **resonate** (rĕz′ə nāt) [*re* <L. "back," "again"]
   intr. v. To produce or show sound vibrations; to echo or resound.

   Rubbing the rim of a crystal glass causes it to **resonate**.

   resonance, *n.*; **resonant**, *adj.*

Challenge Words
assonance
dissonance

7. **sonic** (sŏn′ĭk)
   adj. Pertaining to sound waves or audible sounds.

   Jets create a **sonic** boom when they break the so-called sound barrier.

Familiar Words
revoke
vocal
vocation
voice
vouch
vowel

VOCO, VOCARE, VOCAVI, VOCATUM
<L. "to call"

8. **advocate** (ăd′və kāt) [*ad* <L. "to," "toward"]
   tr. v. To speak in favor of something; to recommend.

   The Mexican rebel Emiliano Zapata **advocated** the rights of peasant farmers against powerful landlords.

   n. A person who argues, supports, or defends a cause.

   The Grimke sisters, Sarah and Angelina, were nineteenth-century **advocates** of political equality for women.

9. **evoke**   (ĭ vōk′)   [*e* = *ex* <L. "from," "out of "]
tr. v. 1. To summon or call forth; to inspire.

The taste of a madeleine, a buttery cookie, **evoked** memories of childhood for the novelist Marcel Proust.

2. To produce a reaction or response.

The shout of "Fire!" **evoked** panic in the audience.

evocation, *n.*; **evocative**, *adj.*

10. **provocative**   (prə vŏk′ə tĭv)   [*pro* <L. "before," "for"]
adj. Exciting; stimulating.

Alice Walker's **provocative** novel about African-American life, *The Color Purple*, was made into an award-winning film.

provocation, *n.*; **provocative**, *adj.*; **provocatively**, *adv.*

11. **vociferous**   (vō sĭf′ər əs)   [*ferre* <L. "to bear"]
adj. Making an outcry; characterized by loudness, especially in protest.

The batter made a **vociferous** protest when the umpire called, "Out!"

vociferate, *v.*; **vociferously**, *adv.*; **vociferousness**, *n.*

EXERCISE 11A

Circle the letter of the best SYNONYM (the word or phrase most nearly the same as the word in bold-faced type).

1. the **redolent** hayloft   a. aromatic   b. musty   c. eerie   d. dark
   e. exhilarating
2. loss of **olfactory** capacity   a. hearing   b. manufacturing
   c. retrospective   d. employment   e. smelling
3. the **sonic** wave   a. electronic   b. extraterrestrial   c. sound
   d. huge   e. jet

Circle the letter of the best ANTONYM (the word or phrase most nearly opposite the word in bold-faced type).

4. to **assimilate** information   a. refuse to take in   b. speculate on
   c. conjugate   d. analyze   e. abhor
5. a(n) **provocative** commercial   a. tasteful   b. dull   c. vulgar
   d. ostentatious   e. irritating
6. the **vociferous** candidate   a. lazy   b. outspoken   c. losing
   d. dishonest   e. mild-mannered
7. a strong **advocate**   a. lawyer   b. extrovert   c. opponent
   d. dislike   e. sense of foreboding

EXERCISE 11B   Circle the letter of the sentence in which the word in bold-faced type is used incorrectly.

1. a. The **resonance** of a seashell causes one to hear the "sound of the sea" when holding it to the ear.
    b. The **resonance** of Isak Dinesen's writing spread beyond her native Denmark.
    c. The **resonance** of her contralto voice can be heard at the far end of the opera house.
    d. Every hour the **resonant** voice of Big Ben, the clock outside the Houses of Parliament, seems to descend over London like leaden circles.

2. a. Are people who **advocate** violence responsible for the violence evoked by their words?
    b. Many doctors **advocate** cutting down on consumption of salt, sugar, and fat.
    c. Henry Ward Beecher, an ardent **advocate** of the abolition of slavery, was the brother of Harriet Beecher Stowe, author of *Uncle Tom's Cabin.*
    d. If I have your **advocate** for the job, I'm sure to get it.

3. a. The English language has **assimilated** many words such as *maize, tepee* and *squash* from Native American languages.
    b. The set designer cleverly **assimilated** snowfall by projecting a video of snow on a scrim, or transparent screen.
    c. The body **assimilates** chemicals through the lungs and skin as well as through the digestive tract.
    d. Friendly and industrious, the new family was quickly **assimilated** into the community.

4. a. **Evoke** me in time for breakfast.
    b. Cultural differences can sometimes **evoke** severe reactions.
    c. Although olfactory memory is subtle, odors can **evoke** powerful emotions.
    d. For many people the sound of an ice cream truck serves as a pleasant **evocation** of childhood summers.

5. a. The lifeguard **admonished** us never to swim alone.
    b. Despite our parents' repeated **admonitions**, we left our bikes unlocked.
    c. I **admonish** you to lend me your homework.
    d. As soon as she set out for her grandmother's house, Little Red Riding Hood forgot her parents' **admonitory** words about not speaking to strangers.

EXERCISE 11C   Fill in each blank with the most appropriate word from Lesson 11. Use a word or any of its forms only once.

1. We need a special _____ commission to investigate these charges against the school board.

2. Hearing their national anthem often _____s tears from Olympic winners as they stand on the victor's block.

3. Although her teacher _____ed her that her grades were slipping, she did not take the warning seriously.

4. Because a piano's wooden frame _____s when it is played, the instrument's tone is intensified.

5. The summer garden was _____ with the odors of roses and lavender.

6. Despite the _____ protests of the crowd, the referee declared the runner out at home base.

7. When whales "sing," they produce _____ patterns that can be heard for many miles underwater.

8. The guest speaker was so _____ that many upset students remained after class to ask questions.

LESSON 12

Noli me tangere.
Touch me not.—John 20:17

Key Words		
assent	presentiment	tactile
contiguous	sensuous	tangent
dissent	sentinel	tangible

SENTIO, SENTIRE, SENSI, SENSUM
<L. "to feel with the senses"

1. **assent**   (ə sĕnt′)   [*as* = *ad* <L. "to"]
   intr. v. To consent; to express agreement (used with *to*).

   Recognizing the need to build new schools, the community **assented** to the higher property tax.

Familiar Words
consent
resent
scent
sensation
sensitive
sensor
sentence
sentry

Challenge Words
sententious
sensate

n. Agreement; consent.

Don't plan our summer vacation until you have the **assent** of the whole family.

Antonym: **dissent**

2. **dissent**   (dĭ sĕnt′)   [*dis* <L. "apart"]
intr. v. To have or express a different opinion.

Because they **dissented** from the established Church of England, the Puritans experienced persecution.

n. Disagreement.

A dictatorship seldom allows **dissent** from its policies to appear in the press.

dissension, *n.*; **dissenter**, *n.*; **dissenting**, *adj.*
Antonym: **assent**

3. **presentiment**   (prĭ zĕn′tə mənt)
[*pre = prae* <L. "before," "in front of"]
n. A sense of something about to happen.

Because I had a **presentiment** that you would call tonight, I knew it was you when the phone rang.

4. **sensuous**   (sĕn′sho͞o əs)
adj. Appealing to the senses, especially aesthetically.

The garden offered much **sensuous** variety of sights, sounds, and smells.

sensuousness, *n.*

5. **sentinel**   (sĕnt′ən əl)
n. A sentry; one who keeps watch.

A **sentinel** was posted at every gate of the besieged city.

TANGO, TANGERE, TETIGI, TACTUM <L. "to touch"

6. **contiguous** (kən tĭg′yōō əs) [*con* <L. "with"]
   adj. Adjoining; sharing a boundary.

   The southern border of Virginia is **contiguous** to North Carolina's northern border.

   contiguity, *n.*; **contiguously**, *adv.*

7. **tangible** (tăn′jə bəl)
   adj. 1. Perceptible by sense of touch.

   Louis Braille developed a system of **tangible** letters by which the blind can read.

   2. Clear and definite; real; concrete.

   Because only a verbal contract had been made, the firm had no **tangible** evidence that they had been cheated.

   tangibleness, *n.*; **tangibility**, *n.*; **tangibly**, *adv.*

Familiar Words
contact
contagious
intact
tact
tactic
taste

Challenge Word
contingent

8. **tactile** (tăk′təl, tăk′tĭl)
   adj. Pertaining to or using the sense of touch; tangible.

   The skin is the largest **tactile** organ of the body.

   tactility, *n.*

9. **tangent** (tăn′jənt)
   adj. 1. Touching.

   One wall of the house was **tangent** with the house next door.

   2. Irrelevant; off the subject.

   Although your comment is interesting, I'm afraid it is **tangent** to the topic of our discussion.

   n. 1. A straight line that touches the outside of a curve but does not cross it.

   For a short distance the highway runs at a **tangent** to the edge of the lake.

   2. A sudden change of direction: "to go off on a tangent."

   She went off on a surprising **tangent**, leaving business school to become a Buddhist nun.

   tangency, *n.*; **tangential**, *adj.*; **tangentially**, *adv.*

EXERCISE 12A Circle the letter of the best SYNONYM (the word or phrase most nearly the same as the word in bold-faced type).

1. to make no **tangible** difference   a. offensive   b. perceptible   c. dangerous   d. auspicious   e. expensive
2. a **presentiment** of danger   a. scorning   b. specter   c. hint   d. foreboding   e. liking
3. to **assent** to a suggestion   a. agree   b. object   c. rise   d. cling   e. refer
4. a **tactile** art form   a. tangible   b. tactful   c. moving   d. redolent   e. provocative

Circle the letter of the best ANTONYM (the word or phrase most nearly opposite the word in bold-faced type).

5. Justice Sandra Day O'Connor's **dissenting** opinion   a. belittling   b. assenting   c. disagreeing   d. resigning   e. reiterating
6. a(n) **tangent** comment   a. touching   b. emotional   c. relevant   d. sensitive   e. clear
7. request **contiguous** parking spaces   a. similar   b. separated   c. ostentatious   d. convenient   e. spacious

EXERCISE 12B Circle the letter of the sentence in which the word in bold-faced type is used incorrectly.

1. a. We often met because our families' front steps were **contiguous**.
   b. Since our dorm rooms were **contiguous**, I overheard their quarrel.
   c. The lawyer's **contiguous** interrogation broke down the witness's alibi.
   d. The artist's studio was **contiguous** to the family's living quarters.
2. a. *Hamlet* opens with the **sentinel's** cry, "Halt, who goes there?"
   b. The peak stands guard over the valley like a **sentinel**.
   c. **Sentinels** at the city gates required the password of everyone who tried to enter.
   d. Even Antigone's tears evoked no **sentinel** of pity from her angry uncle, Creon.
3. a. I recall the **sensuous** experience of going barefoot in the grass.
   b. Young children find **sensuous** pleasure in playing in mud and water.
   c. Some people feel that an opera, because it appeals to both the eye and the ear, is much more **sensuous** than a symphony.
   d. Under hypnosis the volunteer lost all **sensuous** awareness.

4. a. The **assent** of Annapurna, which had never been climbed before, took six days.
    b. Unless you **assent**, no one may enter your home without a warrant.
    c. Congress must **assent** before a president can declare war.
    d. Your promotion has received the board's unanimous **assent**.

5. a. On crashing the Capulets' party, Romeo experiences a strong **presentiment** of disaster.
    b. Before he arrived, the suitor sent his lady **presentiments** of his affection.
    c. Ignoring his **presentiments** of danger, Sir Patrick Spens directed the crew to set sail.
    d. In 1916 Czarina Alexandra had a **presentiment** that if her husband went to the front, the Romanov dynasty would fall.

6. a. Stick to your own project and don't go off on a **tangent** whenever you hear about other interesting ideas.
    b. Although this report is fascinating, I'm afraid it is **tangential** to our investigation.
    c. Because the walls of the prisoners' cells were **tangent**, they could communicate by tapping in code.
    d. A touch of curry added a **tangent** flavor to the stew.

EXERCISE 12C

Fill in each blank with the most appropriate word from Lesson 12. Use a word or any of its forms only once.

1. The blind develop very acute _____ sensitivity, their sense of touch somewhat replacing their sense of sight.

2. Though many claim to have sighted UFOs, almost no _____ evidence has been offered to prove these occurrences.

3. To demonstrate their _____ from the union's decision, a group of workers went on an unauthorized "wild cat" strike.

4. Since their property was _____ , the neighbors agreed to share the expense of a new fence.

5. At every gate the commander of the fort posted a(n) _____ to watch for an attack.

REVIEW EXERCISES FOR LESSONS 11 AND 12

1 Fill in the blanks or circle the letter of the best answer. Do not use a word or root twice.

1. *Account, aggression, arrest,* and *assist* all derive from the prefix

   _____, which means _____ or _____.

2. *tangere* : finger : : *olere* : _____

3. A submarine's *sonar* system determines depth by sending out sound waves and measuring the time taken for them to return. The word

   sonar clearly derives from the root _____, which means

   _____.

4. *Vocation, vocal,* and *revoke* all derive from the root _____,

   which means _____.

5. sentinel : vigilant : :
   a. cook : redolent
   b. musician : resonate
   c. advocate : supportive
   d. specter : speculative
   e. visionary : visible

6. olfactory : redolent : :
   a. taste : vociferous
   b. touch : ticklish
   c. sound : evocative
   d. sight : presentiment
   e. touch : ad hoc

7. Although his parents _____ his participation in football, they _____ him for not studying hard enough.
   a. resonated . . . evoked
   b. dissented to . . . assimilated
   c. improvised . . . provoked
   d. resented . . . reiterated
   e. assented to . . . admonished

8. She had a(n) _____ _____ before the race that she was going to win.
   a. dissenting evocation
   b. tactile refutation
   c. visionary provocation
   d. auspicious presentiment
   e. tactile admonition

2   Matching: On the line at the left, write the letter of the word that best
describes the person(s) or thing in the left-hand column.

_____ **1.** A cat who just fought with a skunk   A. tactile

_____ **2.** An affectionate couple holding hands   B. olfactory

_____ **3.** A newcomer made to feel like   C. sentinel
"one of the family"
D. vociferous

_____ **4.** A watchful chaperon   E. redolent

_____ **5.** A fan who cries, "Kill the umpire!"   F. tangent

G. assimilated

3   Writing or Discussion Activities

1. Write a sentence describing a situation for which an *ad hoc* group
might be formed in your school or community. Use *ad hoc* in your
sentence.
2. Write sentences using any *two* words from each group.
a. admonish, provocative, sentinel, vociferous
b. evoke, assent, dissent, assiduous
3. Describe in a brief paragraph a situation in which you or someone
you know has had a *presentiment* that later proved true. If you cannot
think of a real-life situation, make one up. Use *presentiment* in your
sentence.

Emotions

LESSON 13

Non est jocus esse malignum.
There is no joke in being spiteful.—HORACE

	Key Words	
assuage	jocular	prodigy
festoon	procrastinate	profane
fete	prodigal	profuse
jeopardy		suave

PRO <L. "before," "for"

1. **procrastinate** (prō krăs′tə nāt, prə krăs′tə nāt)
   [*crastinus* <L. "of tomorrow"]
   v. To put off doing something; to delay needlessly.

   Because I **procrastinated** so long, I missed the deadline to register to vote.

   procrastinating, *adj.*; **procrastination**, *n.*; **procrastinator**, *n.*

2. **prodigal**   (prŏd'ĭ gəl)   [*agere* <L. "to drive"]
   adj. 1. Recklessly wasteful; extravagant.

   You'll never live within your income unless you give up your **prodigal** spending.

   2. Profuse; lavish.

   The performance of traditional Hopi dances won **prodigal** praise from the audience.

   n. A spendthrift.

   Although previously thrifty, he became a **prodigal** once he inherited the estate.

   prodigality, *n.*; **prodigally**, *adv.*

3. **prodigy**   (prŏd'ə jē)
   [*prodigum* <L. "prophetic sign," "marvel"]

   n. A person with exceptional talent or powers.

   Wang Yani, a Chinese *prodigy*, won fame for her animal paintings created when she was under ten years of age.

   prodigious, *adj.*; **prodigiously**, *adv.*

4. **profane**   (prō fān', prə fān')   [*fanum* <L. "temple"]
   adj. 1. Showing disrespect toward God or sacred things.

   Their **profane** use of the cathedral for a rock concert offended the entire community.

   2. Nonreligious in subject, form, or use.

   Although the later works of the English writer John Donne are sermons and serious religious verse, his youthful creations are witty and **profane** love poems.

   tr. v. To treat with irreverence.

   You **profane** a mosque by entering it with shoes on.

   profanely, *adv.*; **profanity**, *n.*

5. **profuse**   (prə fyo͞os', prō fyo͞os')   [*fundere* <L. "to pour fourth"]
   adj. Plentiful, prodigal, overflowing; giving abundantly (usually used with *in*).

   Theater critics were **profuse** in their praise for Lillian Hellman's play *The Little Foxes*.

   profusely, *adv.*; **profuseness**, *n.*; **profusion**, *n.*

Familiar Words
jewel
joke
juggler

Challenge Words
jocose
jocund

JOCUS <L. "joke"

6. jeopardy (jĕp′ər dē) [*pars* <L. "part"]
n. Danger; peril.

His crash diet put his health in **jeopardy**.

jeopardize, *v.*

7. jocular (jŏk′yə lər)
adj. Joking; avoiding seriousness.

Your **jocular** attitude is out of place in this serious discussion.

jocularity, *n.*; **jocularly**, *adv.*

SUAVIS <L. "delightful"

8. assauge (ə swāj′) [*as = ad* <L. "to," "toward," "for"]
tr. v. To soothe; to make less severe; to satisfy.

The teacher **assuaged** the children's fears of the storm by explaining the causes of thunder and lightning.

assauged, *adj.*; **assuagement**, *n.*; **assuasive**, *adj.*

9. suave (swäv)
adj. Smooth in social manner.

Accustomed to the social life of an embassy, the ambassador's children were unusually **suave**.

suavely, *adv.*; **suaveness**, *n.*; **suavity**, *n.*

Familiar Words
feast
festival
festive
festivity
fiesta

Challenge Words
festal
festschrift
fete
gabfest

FESTUS <L. "festive"

10. festoon (fĕ stōōn′)
n. A decorative chain of flowers, leaves, or ribbons hung in a curve.

Festoons of oak leaves and gold ribbons were hung around the dining room for Thanksgiving.

tr. v. To decorate with hanging ornaments.

Medals and campaign ribbons **festooned** the general's uniform.

festooned, *adj.*

11. fete (fāt, fĕt)
n. A party or festival, especially one held out of doors.

The city sponsors a Labor Day **fete** at the lake.

tr. v. To give a party in someone's honor.

We **feted** our grandparents in honor of their fiftieth wedding anniversary.

feted, *adj.*

EXERCISE 13A   Circle the letter of the best SYNONYM (the word or phrase most nearly the same as the word in bold-faced type).

1. his **suave** manner   a. insulting   b. introspective   c. awkward
   d. sensuous   e. sophisticated
2. receive a(n) **prodigal** allowance   a. profuse   b. provocative
   c. reliable   d. mean   e. ostensible
3. to **assuage** their doubts   a. soothe   b. mock   c. increase
   d. reiterate   e. admonish

Circle the letter of the best ANTONYM (the word or phrase most nearly opposite the word in bold-faced type).

4. to **profane** her memory   a. curse   b. honor   c. protect   d. disagree
   with   e. jeopardize
5. **profuse** bleeding   a. steady   b. excessive   c. slight   d. occasional
   e. necessary
6. to **festoon** the gym   a. clutter up   b. profane   c. decorate
   d. compliment   e. modify
7. to place **in jeopardy**   a. in suspense   b. in doubt   c. in safekeeping
   d. out of sight   e. beyond reach
8. habitual **procrastination**   a. depression   b. promptness   c. lying
   d. exaggeration   e. vigilance

EXERCISE 13B   Circle the letter of the sentence in which the word in bold-faced type is used incorrectly.

1. a. In Jesus' parable of the **Prodigal** Son, a young man wastes his
      inheritance.
   b. At a potlatch, a ceremonial feast held among Native Americans
      of the Pacific Northwest, **prodigal** hosts may bestow gifts
      amounting to an entire fortune.
   c. Struggling to find escape from her dull life as a village doctor's
      wife, Emma Bovary became a **prodigal**, buying fancy clothes and
      furnishings on borrowed money.
   d. Don't **prodigal** electricity! Turn off the lights when you leave the
      room.

2. a. We **festooned** the classroom with crepe paper streamers.
    b. My cousin, who behaves like a jocular **festoon**, embarrasses me.
    c. The villagers **festooned** the streets with bunting and flags for the Fourth of July parade.
    d. **Festoons** of ivy decorated the dining hall for the banquet.
3. a. They relish **profane** gossip about their neighbors.
    b. However excellent its quality, we are offended to find **profane** art in a temple.
    c. The general's widow withheld from biographers information that she feared would **profane** his reputation.
    d. Expressions that use the name of God casually are considered **profanity**.
4. a. A mathematical **prodigy**, she was doing geometry at five and calculus at ten.
    b. Paul Bunyan was said to have a **prodigious** appetite; he could eat two hundred pancakes for breakfast.
    c. Her friends and neighbors in the *favelas,* or slums, didn't realize that Carolina Maria de Jesus was a literary **prodigy** whose diary would become Brazil's all-time bestseller.
    d. How did such a **prodigy**, who never pays his bills, ever get a credit card?
5. a. With his strong, athletic build and fine coordination he is naturally **jocular**.
    b. Despite her **jocularity**, I knew something was bothering her.
    c. Bugs Bunny often turns to Elmer Fudd and asks **jocularly**, "Eh, what's up Doc?"
    d. The director's **jocular** good humor helped dispel our stage fright on opening night.

EXERCISE 13C   Fill in each blank with the most appropriate word from Lesson 13. Use a word or any of its forms only once.

1. Because of heavy rain, the _____ had to be moved into the gym.

2. She _____d her reputation by plagiarizing a term paper.

3. Although shy, he adopted a(n) _____, sophisticated pose when he went off to college.

4. The princess could _____ Rumpelstiltskin only by promising him her baby if she could not guess his name.

5. Although I usually _____, this time I've finished my report a week early.

6. After being stranded in the Sierra through the winter, the survivors

of the Donner Party greeted their rescuers with _____

thanks and relief.

7. Because he was so late in learning to talk, Albert Einstein's parents

never suspected he was a mathematical _____.

LESSON 14

Volens et potens.
Willing and able.

Key Words		
condole	irate	volition
doleful	ire	zeal
irascible	malevolent	zealot

Familiar Word
Dolores

Challenge Words
dole
dolor
dolorous

DOLEO, DOLERE, DOLUI, DOLITUM
<L. "to grieve"

1. condole (kən dōl′)   [*con = cum* <L. "with"]
intr. v. To express sympathy (used with *with*)

The house was full of neighbors who had
come to **condole** with the grieving family.

condolence, *n.*; **condolent**, *adj.*

2. doleful (dōl′fəl)
adj. Mournful; sad.

I knew by the team's **doleful** expressions that they had lost the
championship.

dolefully, *adv.*; **dolefulness**, *n.*

IRA <L. "anger"

3. irascible (ĭ răs′ə bəl, ī răs′ə bəl)
adj. Irritable; hot tempered.

Although a kindly man, Dr. Samuel Johnson grew **irascible** on the subject of how wealthy patrons neglect writers.

irascibility, *n*.; **irascibly**, *adv*.

4. **irate**   (ī rāt′, ī′rāt)
   adj. Angry; enraged.

   When we got home at two in the morning, our **irate** parents were waiting at the door.

   irately, *adv*.

5. **ire**   (īr)
   n. Anger; rage.

   Unable to control his **ire** at the Israelites' golden calf, Moses smashed the Tablets of the Law.

VOLO, VELLE, VOLUI <L. "to wish"

6. **malevolent**   (mə lĕv′ə lənt)
   [*male* <L. "ill"]
   adj. Wishing harm to others; malicious.

   His **maleovent** gossip created hurt feelings and division in the class.

   malevolence, *n*.; **malevolently**, *adv*.

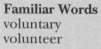

7. **volition**   (və lĭsh′ən)
   n. A conscious choice; use of one's will to make a decision.

   In order to save the life of a friend, Sydney Carton goes to the guillotine of his own **volition**.

   volitional, *adj*.

ZELOS <G. "zeal"

8. **zeal**   (zēl)
   n. Passionate devotion to a cause; ardor.

   Despite being deaf and blind, Helen Keller's **zeal** to learn led her to attend Radcliffe College.

   zealotry, *n*.; **zealous**, *adj*.; **zealously**, *adv*.

9. **zealot**   (zēl′ət)
   n. A zealous person; a fanatic.

Zealots for wildlife protection scattered nails in front of logging trucks to protect logging in national forests.

NOTA BENE: Although the connotations of *zeal* are positive, the word **zealot** conveys the negative meaning of a fanatic, a person who carries zeal to extremes.

Historically *Zealot* describes a member of a Jewish sect during the first century A.D. who opposed a Roman authority in Judea, the area of contemporary Israel, and tried to preserve traditional Jewish law and custom. Used this way, *Zealot* has very positive connotations.

EXERCISE 14A

Circle the letter of the best SYNONYM (the word or phrase most nearly the same as the word in bold-faced type).

1. act with **volition**   a. reluctance   b. ostentation   c. introspection
   d. conscious choice   e. zeal
2. a(n) **irate** customer   a. ostensible   b. frequent   c. furious
   d. vigilant   e. provocative
3. a political **zealot**   a. activist   b. leader   c. visionary   d. specter
   e. fanatic
4. poorly concealed **ire**   a. rage   b. impatience   c. malevolence
   d. jealousy   e. boredom

Circle the letter of the best ANTONYM (the word or phrase most nearly opposite the word in bold-faced type).

5. a(n) **doleful** report   a. generous   b. exclusive   c. prodigal
   d. brief   e. joyful
6. a(n) **irascible** disposition   a. good-natured   b. introspective
   c. irritable   d. changeable   e. sad
7. **malevolent** intentions   a. provocative   b. dangerous   c. far-reaching
   d. irrelevant   e. benevolent
8. to participate with **zeal**   a. indifference   b. skill   c. reticence
   d. vigilance   e. jocularity

EXERCISE 14B

Circle the letter of the sentence in which the word in bold-faced type is used incorrectly.

1. a. He traveled for days to offer his personal **condolences** to his friend's widow.
   b. Although I **condole** with your disappointment, I urge you not to give up hope.

    c. Despite the many suitors who urged her to remarry, Penelope waited **condolently** for Odysseus's return.

    d. Hundreds of **condolent** letters and cards poured in to the bereaved parents.

2. a. We never suspected the guide's friendliness came from a **malevolent** intention to rob us.

    b. You can improve your **malevolent** grades if you'll only study.

    c. In Dickens's *A Tale of Two Cities*, Madame Defarge **malevolently** plans her revenge on French aristocrats.

    d. Police suspect the vandalism was an act of **malevolence** toward the school.

3. a. When Prince Edward finally came to the throne after living in the shadow of his mother, Queen Victoria, he hardly knew how to exercise his own **volition**.

    b. You have no **volition** here; you must follow instructions precisely without question.

    c. Did you act on your own **volition** in this decision, or did your friends influence you?

    d. I know you didn't **volition** to attend this school, but try to make the best of the experience.

4. a. In their **zeal** to bring about revolutionary change in Russia, the Bolsheviks overthrew the moderate Duma, the elected assembly.

    b. Gloria Dean Scott worked **zealously** to bring more children from minority groups into scouting when she was president of the Girl Scouts of America.

    c. Don't be so **zealous** of their championship; work hard to improve your own game.

    d. The **zealotry** of groups who opposed the use of alcohol led in 1919 to the Eighteenth Amendment to the U.S. Constitution, which banned the manufacture and sale of alcoholic beverages in the United States.

EXERCISE 14C   Fill in each blank with the most appropriate word from Lesson 14. Use a word or any of its forms only once.

1. The voters expressed their _____ at the mayor's dishonesty by voting her out of office at the next election.

2. At first dismissed as impractical _____s, advocates of women's suffrage proved their political skill when women gained the vote in 1920.

3. Although I rarely lose my temper, their insults made me so

_____ that I left without saying goodbye.

4. Her _____ for excellence and her years of work and competition have led to a place on the Olympic gymnastics team.

5. Until his transforming Christmas Eve dream, Ebenezer Scrooge was

   a(n) _____ miser, feared and disliked by everyone

   for his irritable personality.

6. Anyone who enjoys a good cry should see this _____
   film.

7. After the guilty verdict, many friends gathered to _____
   with the prisoner's parents.

8. I loathed dancing school and would never have set foot on a dance

   floor of my own _____.

REVIEW EXERCISES FOR LESSONS 13 AND 14

1   Fill in the blanks or circle the letter of the best answer.

1. *Pro* in the word *project* means _____; *pro* in the word

   pronoun means _____.

2. The root in *feast, festive,* and *fiesta* is _____, which means

   _____.

3. *dolere* : *velle* : : to suffer : _____

4. The root in *joke, jocular,* and *jewel* is _____, which means

   _____.

5. assauge : ire : :
   a. satisfy : dissatisfaction
   b. condole : condolence
   c. procrastinate : prodigal
   d. soothe : anger
   e. profane : profusion

6. zeal : zealot : :
   a. waste : prodigal
   b. fame : prodigy
   c. joke : jocular
   d. jeopardy : joker
   e. ostensible : ostentatious

7. To decorate for the fete, we _____ the garden _____.
   a. assauged . . . jocularly
   b. jeopardized . . . zealously
   c. condoled . . . provocatively
   d. improvised . . . prodigiously
   e. festooned . . . profusely

8. Despite her _____ manner at dinner, I knew she was still

   _____ about my podigality.
   a. doleful . . . zealous
   b. irascible . . . malevolent
   c. jocular . . . irate
   d. profane . . . suave
   e. assuaging . . . procrastinating

2 Matching: On the line at the left, write the letter of the word that best fits the person described in the left-hand column.

_____ **1.** Money burns a hole in his pocket   A. zealous

_____ **2.** The life of the party   B. doleful

_____ **3.** Mad as a wet hen   C. irate

_____ **4.** A city slicker   D. profane

_____ **5.** An eager beaver   E. prodigal

   F. suave

   G. jocular

3 Writing or Discussion Activities

1. Write a sentence giving advice to a friend who tends to *procrastinate.*
2. Describe in a sentence a situation that might make you *irascible.* Use *irascible* in your sentence.
3. Describe in a few sentences someone you know whom you consider a *prodigy.* Use *prodigy* in one of the sentences.
4. Write sentences using any *two* words from each group.
   a. ire, assuage, jeopardy, zealous
   b. doleful, jocular, coalition, prodigal
5. Explain how the prefix and root in *condole* contribute to its meaning.

LESSONS 15 AND 16

The Shapes of Things

LESSON 15

Redit agricolis labor actus in orbem.
The farmer's work returns in a circle.—VIRGIL

Key Words		
circuitous	configuration	figurative
circumference	cyclic	orb
circumspect	encyclopedic	orbit

Familiar Words
circle
circuit
circular
circulate
circumstance
circumvent
circus

CIRCUM <L. "around"

1. **circuitous** (sər kyo͞oʹə təs)
   adj. Roundabout; indirect.

   Driven off course by storms and deterred by adventures, Aeneas travels from Troy to Rome in a **circuitous** journey around the Mediterranean.

   circuitously, *adv.*; **circuitousness**, *n.*; **circuitry**, *n.*

2. **circumspect** (sûrʹkəm spĕkt) [*spectare* <L. "to look at"]
   adj. Cautious and watchful; prudent.

Challenge Words
circa
circlet
circumambulate
circumlocation
circumlunar
circumsolar
cirque

Despite her mother's reminder to be **circumspect** on the way to Grandmother's house, Little Red Riding Hood reveals her destination to the ostensibly friendly wolf.

circumspection, *n.*; **circumspectly**, *adv.*

3. **circumference**   (sər kŭm fər əns)   [*ferre* <L. "to carry"]
   n. The outer boundary of a circle; the perimeter.

An ancient defensive wall still stands unbroken on the **circumference** of the French town of Carcassonne, encircling its medieval city limits.

circumferential, *adj.*

NOTA BENE: The prefix *circum* appears in more than twenty-five words listed in most dictionaries. In many words, *circum* is joined to a noun suffix that names the thing around which something moves or exists. For example:
- *circumlunar*—"around the moon"
- *circumsolar*—"around the sun"
- *circumpolar*—"around the pole"
- *circumterrestrial*—"around the earth"

In a large number of words, *circum* is followed by a verb suffix that shows the action by which something moves "around":
- *circumambulate*—"to walk around"
- *circumlocation*—literally "talking around" or "using roundabout language"
- *circumrotate*—literally "to roll around" or "rotate"
- *circumspect*—literally "to look around" or "be cautious"
- *circumvent*—literally "to come around" or "overcome"

ORBIS <L. "circle," "anything round"
ORBITA <L. "wheel"

Challenge Word
orbicular

4. **orbit** (ôr′bĭt)
   n. 1. Path of one body as it revolves around another body.

Several dozen human-made satellites are now in **orbit** around the Earth.

2. A sphere of influence; a range of action or experience.

Since the death of her husband, Martin Luther King, Jr., the **orbit** of Coretta Scott King's influence has increased to make her one of America's most important women.

orbital, *adj.*; **orbiter**, *n.*

5. **orb**   (ôrb)

n. 1. A sphere; anything spherical in shape
(for example, a planet, an eye).

To astronauts observing from outer space,
Earth looks like a blue-green **orb**.

2. A globe carried by a monarch as a symbol
of office.

At her coronation Queen Elizabeth II was invested
with the crown, scepter, and **orb** of Great Britain.

FIGURA <L. "form," "shape"

6. **configuration**   (kən fĭg´yə rā´shən)   [*con = cum* <L. "with"]
n. A shape or outline; a method of arrangement.

To encourage conversation, they arranged the chairs in **configurations**
of six or eight.

configurational, *adj.*

7. **figurative**   (fĭg´yər ə tĭv)
adj. Using figures of speech; symbolic, not literal.

Unless one has a fatal foot disease, "My feet are killing me" is a
figurative expression.

figuratively, *adv.*;   **figurativeness**, *n.*

KUKLOS <G. "wheel," "circle"

8. **cyclic**   (sī´klĭk, sîk´lĭk)
adj. Occurring or moving in cycles.

Because it moves around the sun in a **cyclic**
pattern that takes approximately 76 years,
the reappearance of Halley's comet can be
calculated precisely.

cyclical, *adj.*;   **cyclically**, *adv.*

9. **encyclopedic**   (ĕn sī klə pē´dĭk)   [*en* <G. "in"; *paideia* <G.
"education"]
adj. Possessing information about many subjects or intensively
about one subject.

Having lived in this town for sixty years, he is an **encyclopedic**
resource for local history.

encyclopedically, *adv.*;   **encyclopedist**, *n.*

EXERCISE 15A   Circle the letter of the best SYNONYM (the word or phrase most nearly the same as the word in bold-faced type).

1. the building's **configuration**   a. construction   b. shape   c. purpose
   d. landscape   e. ideology
2. the **circumference** of the forest   a. setting   b. outer edge   c. form
   d. total area   e. sphere
3. a perfect **orb**   a. circle   b. gemstone   c. form   d. circumference
   e. sphere

Circle the letter of the best ANTONYM (the word or phrase most nearly opposite the word in bold-faced type).

4. a(n) **encyclopedic** understanding   a. scholarly   b. prejudiced
   c. ignorant   d. rote   e. sympathetic
5. to inquire **circuitously**   a. directly   b. prejudiciously
   c. ignorantly   d. malevolently   e. quickly
6. a reputation for **circumspection**   a. recklessness   b. losing things
   c. self-centeredness   d. generosity   e. ire
7. a(n) **figurative** statement   a. circumspect   b. blunt   c. imaginative
   d. literal   e. irate

EXERCISE 15B   Circle the letter of the sentence in which the word in bold-faced type is used incorrectly.

1. a. None of the planets' **orbits** around the sun is perfectly circular.
   b. Satellites in **orbit** around the earth now relay television signals
      and report on weather conditions.
   c. Although the **orbit** of her social life has been severely limited
      since her illness, extensive reading has given her a deeper
      understanding of the world.
   d. Our **orbit** to school takes us conveniently past the candy store.
2. a. Romantic poets have sometimes referred to eyes as emerald **orbs**.
   b. Among the treasures of the Holy Roman Empire is an **orb** carried
      by emperors on state occasions since the twelfth century.
   c. The path of Mars around the sun is an elongated **orb**.
   d. Archaeologists uncovered a mysterious stone **orb** that proved to
      be a dinosaur's fossilized egg.
3. a. Tides are **cyclic** with two flood tides and two ebb tides in
      approximately 24 hours.
   b. Because gasoline and automobile tires were scarce during World
      War II, many Americans rediscovered the bicycle and began to
      travel **cyclically**.
   c. Many cultures regard time as **cyclical**, with similar events
      recurring in different eras rather than once and for all.

    d. People in tropical climates do not experience the **cyclic** nature of the seasons as dramatically as people in temperate zones.

4. a. Young children are often alarmed by adult **figurativeness**, such as statements like "I'm so hungry I could eat a horse."

    b. **Figurative** language includes personifications like "the wind screamed" and metaphors like "the wind was a scream."

    c. Ballet dancers must be extremely **figurative**, both in strength and flexibility.

    d. My parents are going to kill me when they see my grades, **figuratively** speaking, of course.

5. a. Driving on **circuitous** roads always makes me car sick.

    b. She approached the topic of a loan **circuitously**, chatting first about the weather, then about how long they had been friends, and finally about her unforeseen educational expenses.

    c. Despite the **circuitry** of our conversation, which never once mentioned business, I became aware that the dealer was ready to sell at my price.

    d. Although this route is more **circuitous** than the highway, it permits you to see more of the countryside.

EXERCISE 15C

Fill in each blank with the most appropriate word from Lesson 15. Use a word or any of its forms only once.

1. The _____ of the constellation Ursa Major is like a bear or a dipper.

2. During the nineteenth century few parts of the world were out of the _____ of British influence.

3. After years of teaching, she has acquired a(n) _____ grasp of French literature.

4. To avoid being followed, we took a(n) _____ route that wandered around town.

5. Although she strives to be as _____ and proper as her aunt requires, Anne of Green Gables often acts impulsively and gets into trouble.

6. Along the _____ of the small park was an elegant wrought-iron fence.

7. Some _____ expressions like "as quick as a wink" and "as smart as a whip" have become cliches, statements worn out with use.

8. Our educational system is _____, with a new year beginning every September and ending every June, followed by a summer vacation.

LESSON 16

Ore rotundo.
With round (eloquent) mouth.

<table>
<tr><td colspan="3" align="center">**Key Words**</td></tr>
<tr><td>cavernous</td><td>feign</td><td>idyll</td></tr>
<tr><td>concave</td><td>feint</td><td>rote</td></tr>
<tr><td>effigy</td><td>ideology</td><td>rotund</td></tr>
<tr><td>excavate</td><td></td><td>rotunda</td></tr>
</table>

Familiar Words
faint
fiction
nonfiction

FINGO, FINGERE, FINXI, FICTIM <L. "to shape"

1. **feign** (fān)
   tr. v. To pretend.

   Although she **feigned** tears at the news, she was secretly delighted.

   feigned, *adj.*

Challenge Word
fictive

2. **feint** (fānt)
   n. 1. A misleading movement or pretended attack.

   The boxer made a **feint** with his left and then struck a surprise blow with his right.

   2. A pretense; a scheme to mislead.

   They set fire as a **feint** to cover their escape.

   tr. v. To make a misleading movement or pretended attack.

   The cavalry **feinted** a charge to draw cannon fire and allow the infantry to advance.

3. **effigy** (ĕf′ə jē) [*ef* = *ex* <L. "from," "out of"]
   n. A sculpture or model of a person.

   Children in England burn **effigies** of Guy Fawkes, an Elizabethan traitor, on November 5.

Familiar Words
idea
idealist
idealize
kaleidoscope

EIDOS <G. "shape," "form"

4. **ideology** (ī′dē ŏl′ə jē, ĭd′dē ŏl′ə jē) [*logos* <G. "word," "speech"]
   n. The main ideas of a class, group, or movement.

Training young people to be prepared in emergencies is an important aspect of Boy Scout and Girl Scout **ideology**.

ideological, *adj.*; **ideologist**, *n.*; **ideologue**, *n.*

NOTA BENE: The word *ideology* can have both positive and negative connotations. Used positively, *ideology* can be a synonym for *creed*, or "belief system":
• Puritan *ideology* put great value on hard work and thriftiness.
   Used negatively, *ideology* suggests inflexible or fanatically-held beliefs:
• Under Joseph Stalin it was more important for Communist party members to be *ideologically* correct than to be professionally capable.
   The word *ideologue*, "a person who advocates an ideology," is almost always negative in connotation.

5. **idyll, idyl**   (īd′l)
   n. 1. A short description of a peaceful or romantic scene, usually of country life.

Life on the American frontier was no **idyll** but full of hard work, loneliness, and physical danger.

2. A peaceful or romantic scene or incident.

The marooned boys in *The Lord of the Flies* expect to enjoy an **idyll** in their tropical island paradise.

idyllic, *adj.*; **idyllically**, *adv.*

ROTA <L. "wheel"
ROTUNDUS <L. "round"

6. **rote**   (rōt)
   n. 1. By memory without thought of the meaning.

Students rarely remember vocabulary words they learn by **rote** and never use in writing or discussion.

2. Mechanical routine.

Assembly lines where one works by **rote** tend to be more tiring than work with varied activities.

rote, *adj.*

7. **rotunda**   (rō tŭn′də)
   n. A circular domed building or hall.

The United States Capitol has a large **rotunda** at its center.

8. **rotund** (rō tŭnd′)
   adj. Plump; rounded.

   Santa Claus was described as a jolly fellow with a **rotund** belly that "shook when he laughed like a bowl full of jelly."

   rotundity, *n.*; **rotundness**, *n.*

CAVEA <L. "a hollow"

Familiar Words
cage
cave
cavity
decoy
excavate

9. **cavernous** (kăv′ər nəs)
   adj. 1. Like a large cave in size or darkness.

   The **cavernous** sports stadium could hold a hundred thousand spectators.

   2. Filled with caves or cavities.

   The **cavernous** cliffs contained many Stone Age burial sites.

10. **concave** (kŏn kāv′, kŏn kāv) [*con* = *cum* <L. "with"]
    adj. Curved like the inner surface of a ball.

    Concave satellite dishes stand outside many homes to improve television reception.

    concavely, *adv.*; **concaveness**, *n.*; **concavity**, *n.*
    Antonym: **convex**

    NOTA BENE: Students often confuse *concave* and *convex*. One way to distinguish these words is to remember that *concave* comes from *cavea* and describes a cave-like shape.

11. **excavate** (ēk′skə vāt) [*ex* <L. "from," "out of"]
    tr. v. To dig out; to make a hole by digging.

    When workers began to **excavate** a new subway tunnel in London, they discovered important Roman and medieval relics.

    excavation, *n.*; **excavator**, *n.*

EXERCISE 16A   Circle the letter of the best SYNONYM (the word or phrase most nearly the same as the word(s) in bold-faced type).

1. a clever **feint**   a. swoon   b. pretense   c. slight   d. reply   e. idea
2. frightened by a(n) **effigy**   a. model of a person   b. rumor   c. configuration   d. prodigy   e. sentinel

3. a resonant **concavity**   a. excavation   b. circumference   c. open
   space   d. hollowed-out place   e. huge area
4. perform **by rote**   a. from written instructions   b. on an ad hoc
   basis   c. by memory   d. in series   e. with assistance

Circle the letter of the best ANTONYM (the word or phrase most nearly
opposite the word in bold-faced type).

5. a(n) **rotund** armchair   a. uncomfortable   b. new   c. shapeless
   d. concave   e. elegant
6. a(n) **idyllic** vacation   a. expensive   b. busy   c. disastrous
   d. solitary   e. prudent
7. their **feigned** surprise   a. complete   b. genuine   c. disappointed
   d. pretended   e. shocked
8. the **excavation** of an archeological site   a. burial   b. exploration
   c. discovery   d. festooning   e. advocation

EXERCISE 16B   Circle the letter of the sentence in which the word in bold-faced type is
used incorrectly.

1. a. We had to **rote** the names and dates of all the presidents.
   b. Most Muslims learn long passages of the Koran by **rote**.
   c. The **rote** work of stamping labels gave her time to dream.
   d. Although he could quote by **rote** from ideological texts, he could
      not explain them.
2. a. The fencer **feinted** to throw his opponent off balance.
   b. Because of their tight corsets, which prevented deep breathing,
      Victorian women frequently **feinted** from lack of breath.
   c. His coughing fit served as a **feint** to distract the guard while his
      cellmate escaped.
   d. We **feinted** an interest in antiques in order to be allowed to
      attend the auction.
3. a. Constable's paintings present an **idyllic** view of the English
      landscape and omit scenes of poverty and discomfort.
   b. The Old Testament forbids the worship of **idylls** and "graven
      images."
   c. Greek poets often set their **idylls** in Arcadia, a beautiful, rural
      landscape.
   d. They recalled their honeymoon in the Alps as an **idyll**.
4. a. No one was fooled by his **feigned** friendliness.
   b. The moral of the story of "the boy who cried wolf" is don't **feign**
      danger.
   c. Although we thought she was only **feigning**, she was truly ill.
   d. You can't **feign** me with your flattering lies!

5. a. The squad worked all day to **concave** the foxhole.
   b. Years of erosion had hollowed out a **concavity** beneath the waterfall.
   c. Puffins nested in the **concave** irregularities of the cliff.
   d. Their cheeks became **concave** from starvation.
6. a. Shaker **ideology** stressed simplicity in all things.
   b. Although she is a loyal Republican, her views on taxation differ **ideologically** from party policy.
   c. Only an **ideologist** like you would always expect the best from everyone.
   d. In defiance of their parents' Communist **ideology**, they favored private enterprise and investment of capital.

EXERCISE 16C Fill in each blank with the most appropriate word from Lesson 16. Use a word or any of its forms only once.

1. The typical American state capitol has a dome with a(n) _____ beneath.

2. Nazi _____ claimed Germans to be racially superior to all other people.

3. Humpty Dumpty's _____ shape resembled an egg.

4. The _____ hangar was large enough to contain four large cargo planes.

5. The Roman city of Pompeii has been _____ d from the volcanic rubble that buried it in A.D. 79.

6. In Thomas Hardy's novel *The Mayor of Casterbridge*, Thomas Henchard is prevented from suicide by drowning when he sees a(n)

_____ of himself that has been thrown into the river.

REVIEW EXERCISES FOR LESSONS 15 AND 16

1 Fill in the blanks or circle the letter of the best answer.

1. circle : *orbis* : :
   a. *circum* : *cavea*
   b. round : around
   c. shape : *figura*
   d. cave : concave
   e. concave : excavate

2. *Circle, circus,* and *circulate* derive from the root _____,

which means _____.

3. Though her work as an extra involved standing in the hot sun all
    day, Celeste was happy just to be within the _____ of her
    favorite movie star.

4. *Cave, excavate,* and *cage* derive from the root _____, which
    means _____.

5. circuitous : direct : :
    a. excavate : rotund
    b. concave : cave
    c. figurative : literal
    d. ideological : idyllic
    e. encyclopedic : dictionary

6. rote : wrote : :
    a. feint : faint
    b. idyll : ideal
    c. plump : rotund
    d. orb : orbit
    e. cyclic : cycle

7. Archaeologists believe the _____ they have _____ to be
    of Tupac Amaru, the last Inca ruler.
    a. orb . . . evoked
    b. concavity . . . condoled
    c. configuration . . . festooned
    d. rotunda . . . orbited
    e. effigy . . . excavated

8. The _____ castle stood in a(n) _____ setting by a mountain
    lake.
    a. figurative . . . jocular
    b. circumspect . . . redolent
    c. cavernous . . . idyllic
    d. rotund . . . doleful
    e. encyclopedic . . . feigned

2 Matching: On the lines at the left, write the letters of two words from the right-hand column that paraphrase the words in the left-hand column.

_____ _____ **1.** An enormous building with a dome

_____ _____ **2.** A regularly recurring archaeological dig

_____ _____ **3.** Pretended prudence

_____ _____ **4.** A plump spokesperson for a belief

_____ _____ **5.** The perimeter of a shape

A. rotund
B. rotunda
C. circumspection
D. cyclic
E. feigned
F. configuration
G. cavernous
H. effigy
I. circumference
J. excavation
K. ideologue
L. idyllic

3 Writing or Discussion Activities

1. Try to explain in a sentence or two the possible relationship between _rote_ and its root, _rota_, meaning "wheel."
2. Think of a situation in which you have needed to be _circumspect_. In a brief paragraph describe this situation and how you acted on it. Were you successful at _circumspection_ or not? Use a form of _circumspect_ in your paragraph.
3. State one idea that is part of the _ideology_ of any group you know of. Use a form of _ideology_ in your sentence.
4. Describe how you might get from your home to school using a _circuitous_ route. Use _circuitous_ in your sentence.
5. Many jokes are based on taking a figurative statement literally. For example:
   Why did the silly man throw a clock out the window? He wanted to see time fly.
   Do one of the following:
   a. Make a list of five jokes that also depend on a literal interpretation of a figurative statement.
   b. Make a list of five sentences in which the meaning is different depending on whether the sentences are understood literally or figuratively.

WORD LIST

(Numbers in parentheses refer to the lesson in which the word appears.)

abhor (7)

abound (7)

abrasive (7)

abscond (7)

absolve (8)

abstain (5)

abstemious (7)

ad hoc (11)

adjunct (6)

admonish (11)

adversity (2)

advocate (11)

analyze (8)

aptitude (6)

ascertain (7)

assent (12)

assimilate (11)

assuage (13)

astringent (6)

auspicious (10)

avert (2)

catalyst (8)

cavernous (16)

circuitous (15)

circumference (15)

circumspect (15)

coherent (5)

colloquial (5)

commiserate (5)

commodious (5)

compound (3)

concave (16)

concise (8)

condole (14)

condone (5)

configuration (15)

conjugate (6)

contend (1)

contiguous (12)

contort (2)

contrite (5)

cyclic (15)

defer (1)

dilatory (1)

discern (7)

discreet (7)

dissent (12)

distort (2)

doleful (14)

effigy (16)

elation (1)

encyclopedic (15)

evoke (11)

excavate (16)

excerpt (3)

exhilarate (3)

exonerate (3)

exorbitant (3)

exposition (3)

expound (3)

extraneous (3)

extraterrestrial (4)

extrovert (4)

feign (16)

feint (16)

festoon (13)

fete (13)

figurative (15)

herbicide (8)

ideology (16)

idyll (16)

impertinent (5)

impose (3)

imposter (3)

improvise (9)

inept (6)

infer (1)

infraction (7)

infringe (7)

injunction (6)

intent (1)

introspection (10)

introvert (2)

irascible (14)

irate (14)

ire (14)

jeopardy (13)

jocular (13)

juncture (6)

malevolent (14)

mediate (4)

mediocrity (4)

medium (4)

non sequitur (4)

obsequious (4)

olfactory (11)

orb (15)

orbit (15)

ostensible (9)

ostentatious (9)

percussion (1)

perennial (1)

permeate (1)

persevere (1)

pertinacious (5)

perverse (2)

precise (8)

presentiment (12)

procrastinate (13)

prodigal (13)

prodigy (13)

profane (13)

profuse (13)

proponent (3)

prose (2)

provocative (11)

redolent (11)

refute (9)

reiterate (9)

repartee (9)

repertoire (9)

repose (9)

resolute (8)

resolve (8)

resonate (11)

reticent (9)

retort (2)

retrospect (10)

rote (16)

rotund (16)

rotunda (16)

sensuous (12)

sentinel (12)

sequester (4)

sonic (11)

specimen (10)

specter (10)

spectrum (10)

speculate (10)

strait (6)

stringent (6)

suave (13)

subjugate (6)

subsequent (4)

subservient (2)

subvert (2)

suffrage (7)

superfluous (8)

superlative (8)

surveillance (10)

tactile (12)

tangent (12)

tangible (12)

tenacity (5)

tortuous (2)

vigil (10)

vigilant (10)

visionary (9)

vociferous (11)

volition (14)

zeal (14)

zealot (14)